Praise for
Every Woman's Marriage
by Shannon and Greg Ethridge

"Finally! An insightful and frank discussion about the perspectives, expectations, and behaviors that impair marital relationships. With Shannon's expertise on sexual and emotional integrity and Greg's male perspective, *Every Woman's Marriage* offers practical guidance for reigniting the intimacy and passion every woman longs for."

—GINGER KOLBABA, managing editor of *Marriage Partnership* magazine and author of *Surprised by Remarriage*

Praise for
Every Woman's Battle
by Shannon Ethridge

"This book sheds light on the often unspoken sensitivities and issues that women wrestle with. Not only is it well written, but it is liberating and refreshing with sound principles for overcoming the things that threaten to keep us from experiencing the fullness of joy that is part of God's big-picture plan for our lives."

—MICHELLE MCKINNEY HAMMOND, author of *In Search of the Proverbs 31 Man* and *The Unspoken Rules of Love*

"In today's permissive culture, it's dangerously easy for even the most principled of women to reason away unhealthy thoughts, attitudes, and flirtations with men who aren't our husbands. In *Every Woman's Battle,* Shannon Ethridge bravely and respectfully draws a line in the sand for all of us. This is a must-read for every woman who desires true intimacy and sexual integrity."

—CONSTANCE RHODES, author of *Life Inside the "Thin" Cage*

"There's a common, almost Victorian, myth that women don't really struggle with sexual sin. That myth causes many women to feel a double shame. The shame of struggling sexually is compounded by the assumption that few, if any, women share the same battle. Shannon Ethridge artfully and boldly unveils the war and offers women a way to enter the battle with courage, hope, and grace. *Every Woman's Battle* will help both men and women comprehend the glorious beauty and sensuality of holiness. This is a desperately needed book."

—DR. DAN B. ALLENDER, president of Mars Hill Graduate School
and author of *The Healing Path* and *To Be Told*

"If you're like me, you want the deepest connection possible with your husband, you want a soul-to-soul connection not encumbered by anything that could damage it—and you're going to find Shannon's book immeasurably helpful in doing just that. *Every Woman's Battle* is the best resource I know for embracing God's plan for sexual and emotional integrity as a woman."

—LESLIE PARROTT, author of *When Bad Things Happen to Good Marriages*

"Many of my *Bad Girls of the Bible* readers have tearfully confessed to me their struggles with sexual sins—promiscuity, adultery, and self-gratification among them. Since we cannot pretend Christian women don't face these temptations, it's a relief to have a sound resource like this one to recommend. Shannon Ethridge's straightforward, nonjudgmental, step-by-step approach can help women come clean in the best way possible—through an intimate relationship with the Lover of their souls."

—LIZ CURTIS HIGGS, best-selling author of *Bad Girls of the Bible, Really Bad Girls of the Bible,* and *Unveiling Mary Magdalene*

every
woman's
marriage
workbook

every woman's marriage workbook

How to Ignite the Joy and Passion You Both Desire

Shannon and Greg Ethridge

WATERBROOK
PRESS

EVERY WOMAN'S MARRIAGE WORKBOOK
PUBLISHED BY WATERBROOK PRESS
12265 Oracle Boulevard, Suite 200
Colorado Springs, Colorado 80921
A division of Random House Inc.

Details in some anecdotes and stories have been changed to protect the identities of the persons involved.

ISBN 1-4000-7163-1

Printed in the United States of America
2006—First Edition

10 9 8 7 6 5 4 3 2 1

contents

questions you may have about this workbook

What will the *Every Woman's Marriage Workbook* do for me?
This workbook will help you go the extra mile in applying the principles presented in *Every Woman's Marriage,* so you can change the things that only you can change for the good of your relationship. You'll discover what you may be doing to cause your husband's flame of joy and passion to die, how to reignite the flame, and how to throw fuel on it for a greatly enhanced marital connection. Through thought-provoking questions and soul-searching exercises, you'll learn how to inspire rather than require the intimacy you long to experience with your husband.

Is this workbook enough, or do I also need a copy of the book *Every Woman's Marriage*?
While this workbook contains excerpts from *Every Woman's Marriage* (each one marked at the beginning and end by this symbol: 📖), you'll need to read the book to see the big picture and get the full effect of the concepts presented.

How much time is required to complete each lesson? Do I need to work through every part of each chapter?
In addition to the time it will take you to read the accompanying chapters in *Every Woman's Marriage,* it will take thirty to forty-five minutes to answer the questions in the workbook. While it's important to work through all the

questions, you may want to spend more time on areas that target your specific needs.

Each chapter contains four parts: Planting Good Seeds (Personally Seeking God's Truth), Weeding Out Deception (Recognizing the Truth), Harvesting Joy and Passion (Applying the Truth), and Growing Together (Sharing the Truth in Small-Group Discussion). The first three parts are intended for individual study. They will help you hide God's Word in your heart, help you recognize and remove things in your life that can hinder joy and passion in your marriage, and help you reap the rewards of deeper levels of marital intimacy and satisfaction. The last part of each chapter is designed especially for group discussion, although it can also be done individually.

How do I organize a group study?

You'll be amazed at how much more you'll get out of the book and workbook if you go through it with a group of like-minded women. I also recommend that husbands form a group to read and discuss the principles presented in the *Every Man's Marriage* book and workbook (by Stephen Arterburn and Fred Stoeker).

If you don't know of an existing group, start one of your own! Whether it's a Sunday-school class or a group of coworkers, neighbors, or friends, invite six to eight women to meet and discuss the book and workbook. Let them know that it will likely take a couple of hours each week to read the chapters in the book and then answer the corresponding questions in the workbook. Most women will recognize that this is a worthwhile investment of their time, and they will eagerly seek practical advice on how to ignite more joy and passion in their relationships with their husbands.

Your group will meet together eight times. Keep each meeting to a reasonable amount of time (I recommend sixty to ninety minutes) so everyone will consider it a blessing rather than a burden. If evenings are not a possibility, consider a weekly breakfast or brown-bag lunch meeting.

When women gather to discuss such an intimate topic as marriage, the temptation to go off on rabbit trails with a variety of other "safer" topics can be overwhelming, especially for those who feel uncomfortable at first. To ensure that the conversation stays on track, designate one person to be the group facilitator. This facilitator has no responsibilities to teach, lecture, or prepare anything in advance, but simply to begin and end the meeting at the designated times and to make sure the conversation is moving along in a productive manner.

Nothing heals like meeting with other women with the goal of removing your masks and talking about the struggles you each face in being the wives you long to be. You never know, perhaps your group will breathe life into someone's otherwise lifeless marriage, or prevent a woman from prematurely giving up on her husband or from falling into an extramarital affair. By learning to inspire from our husbands the intimacy we long for, we can affair-proof our relationships and divorce-proof our families like never before.

Love takes two to tango,
and as much as we want to throw stones
at our clumsy partners,
we all need to stop and ask ourselves,
What part do I play in my marriage's dance of discontentment?

—from chapter 2 of *Every Woman's Marriage*

when hearts grow cold

Read chapters 1 and 2 in *Every Woman's Marriage.*

PLANTING GOOD SEEDS
(Personally Seeking God's Truth)

As you seek to discover how to ignite the joy and passion you and your husband desire in your relationship, here is a good seed to plant in your heart:

> Consider the blameless, observe the upright;
>> there is a future for the [woman] of peace. (Psalm 37:37, NIV)

1. Prior to your wedding day, how did you envision your future with your husband? How has your reality measured up to your fantasy of marriage?

2. Have there been times when you felt desperate to change your husband, to change yourself, or to resolve a situation that was robbing you of peace in the relationship? What could God have been trying to teach you through these experiences?

> When a [woman's] ways are pleasing to the LORD,
>   he makes even [her] enemies live at peace with [her].
> Better a little with righteousness
>   than much gain with injustice.
> In [her] heart a [woman] plans [her] course,
>   but the LORD determines [her] steps. (Proverbs 16:7–9, NIV)

3. Do you believe your future together could be more joyful and passionate if you learn how to move from desperation to dependence upon the Lord? Why or why not?

4. What, specifically, can you do to make your ways of relating with your husband more pleasing to God? Give examples of what this may look like and what you hope the results of such actions will be.

⚘ WEEDING OUT DECEPTION
(Recognizing the Truth)

📖 I was constantly badgering Greg for not initiating romance anymore, for being too laid back. I had a long list of complaints: He never called me up for a date or offered to take me out to dinner. He didn't send cards or bring me flowers. I was weary of having to hint around for my emotional needs to be met, and I felt it didn't count if he didn't come up with the idea of how to do so himself. I was sick and tired of always picking up LEGOs and Tinkertoys, wiping children's noses and behinds, cleaning Goldfish and Cheerios out of the minivan seats, and feeling as if there had to be more to life.

With each passing day, I slipped deeper into depression. In hindsight, I realize that my unhappiness wasn't about what my husband was or wasn't doing; rather, it was about how I felt about myself. I needed Greg to affirm me, to make me feel beautiful, and to convince me that I was desirable, because I didn't know how to feel any of these things on my own. But at the time, I felt sure that he was to blame. 📖

5. Have you ever felt there must be more to life and been tempted to place the blame on your husband rather than taking responsibility for your own happiness? If so, describe one such memory and how you felt at the time.

6. In hindsight, what do you think your husband should have been doing to make you feel better during this time? Would it have truly been enough to satisfy you and give you a genuine sense of peace and happiness?

7. What things could you have been doing to make yourself feel better during that season of life? If you could go back, what would you do differently?

8. The next time you experience a deep sense of disappointment and disillusionment in your life or marriage, how can you avoid placing the blame on your husband and take responsibility for your own peace and contentment? What will you do to avoid playing the blame game?

    📖 After only one year of marriage, it's clear that Claire's reality isn't measuring up to her expectations. She laments: "We're usually either fighting or not talking much at all. The word *divorce* isn't in our vocabularies, but I frequently have thoughts about what my life could be like after my husband dies. I have a mental list of men I'd date. It's pretty long. They have all met different needs at different times. Then I think of how wonderful it would be to be single again. I'd be better off without his college debt and dirty socks. But I married him for a reason. What was it?"

Ironically, Claire also recalls that she was miserable as a single woman and thought that getting married would solve all her problems. As her situation illustrates, getting rid of your single status only exchanges one set of problems for another, more complex set of problems. 📖

9. Do you ever long to be single again? If so, what new problems would be created by your divorced or widowed status (socially, financially, relationally, emotionally, and so on)? Do you really prefer those problems to the ones you have experienced in your marriage?

10. Have you been tempted to buy into the lie that if you had a different man, your life would be better? Is this a realistic expectation—that a different person would solve your problems? Why or why not?

🐚 HARVESTING JOY AND PASSION
(Applying the Truth)

📖 Let's face it. Nothing magical happens once we put those rings on our fingers. If we were unhappy before marriage, chances are we'll go back to being unhappy shortly after the honeymoon. Marriage doesn't make us feel better about ourselves or solve our problems in the long run. No husband can be the White Knight who rescues us from all our issues and insecurities. At some point we

have to put on our "big-girl panties" and go through the work
of resolving our own issues, remedying our own insecurities, and
becoming happy with ourselves before we can truly be happy in
marriage. 📖

11. What personal issues do you struggle with that have added to the stress
in your marriage relationship?

12. What work do you sense you may need to do to resolve these issues or
insecurities and become truly happy with yourself? Might you need to
enlist the help of others? If so, how?

📖 Too often we wives seem to assume that our husbands' hearts
are made of steel. Perhaps the rings we wear on our fingers give us
the impression that regardless of how we treat them, they'll always
be by our sides.

I don't know about you, but I don't want a husband who is
physically alive but emotionally dead toward me. I want Greg to
be excited about our relationship and to look forward to coming
home every day. I don't want him going through the motions to
jump through my hoops just to keep me off his back. I want his
heart to remain soft and warm toward me. However, I've come to
realize that I can't have these things while taking him for granted
and treating him disrespectfully, both of which I have done many
times in the past. 📖

13. What about you? Do you share this desire—to have your husband look forward to coming home every day with a soft, warm heart toward you? How can you inspire this reaction in him?

14. What specific behaviors or attitudes will you strive to avoid to keep his heart from growing cold toward you?

❧ GROWING TOGETHER
(Sharing the Truth in Small-Group Discussion)

> 📖 *"You just don't meet my emotional needs!"*
>
> After seven years of marriage, I was actually thinking of leaving Greg and my two young children in pursuit of the "love" I felt entitled to but didn't feel I was getting in our relationship. I had no idea where I would go or how I would make it on my own, but I wasn't sure I could survive a lifeless marriage. I felt like I was nothing more than a maid, cook, nanny, and occasional outlet for sexual tension, positions for which I was sadly underpaid. 📖

15. Have you ever thought you weren't getting the "love" you felt entitled to or that your husband was taking you for granted? How did this make you feel? Why?

📖 The truth is, no marriage is exempt from disillusionment. Even the brightest relationship has dark days clouding a couple's history together, raining on their "we have the perfect marriage" parade. On the exterior, a wife may appear to have the ideal marriage, but the interior landscape of her heart often reveals deep disappointment, anger, bitterness, and regret. 📖

16. Have you believed that your marital struggles are unique? If so, how does it make you feel to know that many other women have similar experiences?

17. Why do you think most couples experience desperate times at some point (or at several points)? What can we learn from this common phenomenon? What hope can this create in us—if we allow it?

📖 It's true that many women aren't happy; it's equally true that many men aren't happy. These *are* desperate times, and perhaps this desperation is an indication that it's time for us women to take desperate measures and ask ourselves, *Am I contributing to the demise of the masculine image by how I treat my husband?* Love takes two to tango, and as much as we want to throw stones at our clumsy partners, we all need to stop and ask ourselves, *What part do I play in my marriage's dance of discontentment?*

The bottom line is this: *Even if you firmly believe that 95 percent of the issues in your marriage are your husband's fault, are you willing to focus on the 5 percent that you do have control over?* 📖

18. For a moment, ignore whatever problems you feel your husband brings into your relationship. Focus strictly on the part *you* play in the dance of discontentment. What areas do you need to work on to reignite joy and passion in your relationship?

19. What specific things can others in the group do to hold you accountable or to encourage you to make positive changes in your ways of relating to your husband?

∞

Dear Lord, we acknowledge that our society is experiencing incredibly desperate times in light of the divorce rates and all of the repercussions of so many broken homes in our world. We don't want to add to this problem. We want to be a part of the solution. We seek Your supernatural guidance in creating rock-solid marriage relationships that will withstand the test of time and be bright rays of light that drive away darkness and illuminate hope in other married couples. Help us to take the desperate measures we need to take to recognize and remedy our own problems. We seek to rediscover peace, contentment, joy, and passion in our marriages, for our own sakes and for the sakes of our husbands, children, and our grandchildren for many generations to come. Amen.

looking at the big picture

Read chapters 3, 4, and 5 in *Every Woman's Marriage.*

🌱 PLANTING GOOD SEEDS
(Personally Seeking God's Truth)

As you reflect on God's creation of marriage, plant Paul's words deep within your heart:

> As the Scriptures say, "A man leaves his father and mother and is joined to his wife, and the two are united into one." This is a great mystery, but it is an illustration of the way Christ and the church are one. (Ephesians 5:31–32)

1. Have you ever pondered the mystery of why God calls you to be joined to your spouse as one inseparable unit? What do you think it means for two to be united into one?

2. Why do you think that an everlasting marriage commitment between two believers is so important to God? Is it as important to you? Why or why not?

3. Are there ways in which you need to focus on being more one with your spouse instead of operating separately or independently of him? If so, how?

As you consider the big-picture purpose of marriage, plant this good seed in your heart:

> You husbands must love your wives with the same love Christ showed the church. He gave up his life for her *to make her holy and clean,* washed by baptism and God's word. He did this to present her to himself as a glorious church without a spot or wrinkle or any other blemish. Instead, she will be holy and without fault. (Ephesians 5:25–27, emphasis added)

4. What difference would it make in a marriage if a husband strove to love his wife as Christ loved the church? Can you identify certain ways that your husband attempts to love you like this? If so, what are they?

5. In what ways does your marriage relationship purify you and make you more holy than when you were single? Are there particular issues in your life that have come to the surface since you've been married, forcing you to deal with them like never before?

As you consider how to love your husband, plant this seed in your heart:

> We know what real love is because Christ gave up his life for us. (1 John 3:16)

6. In what ways have you and your husband given up your lives for each other?

7. In what ways do you still need to give up your life for the sake of your husband and for unity in your marriage?

🥄 WEEDING OUT DECEPTION
(Recognizing the Truth)

📖 James seemed attentive and sounded ideal. Andrea raved about how he called several times each day just to see what she was doing, how he said the sweetest things to her, and how he continued to assure her that he (and their relationship) was truly the real deal. When Greg would call me on my cell phone, it was to talk about where each kid had to be that day or to ask what he could make for supper. He said "I love you" before we hung up, but it wasn't magical. It didn't inspire any change in my tone of voice. No sweaty palms. No butterflies in my stomach. Just a routine conversation. Our relationship hasn't always been this way. There was a time when I did backflips whenever he called.

After I hung up, I made a mental note: *Guard your heart, Shannon!* I had to be careful not to be jealous of the intensity of Andrea's new relationship. I couldn't compare my marriage of fifteen years to this fifteen-day-old relationship. Maybe Greg and I didn't have the flame of intensity anymore, but we had something far more brilliant—the glowing embers of intimacy.📖

8. Do you ever lament because your husband no longer gives you sweaty palms or butterflies in your stomach? If so, how has this made you feel?

9. After reading part 2 of *Every Woman's Marriage,* do you agree that sweaty palms, butterflies, and fireworks aren't good indicators of relational success? Why or why not?

10. What are more accurate indicators of marital success? List as many as you can think of. As you look over your list, underline the indicators that are present in your marriage, then circle those that you'd like to strive to work on.

      📖 So when Greg looked into my heart, what did he see that no one else could? He saw a hurting little girl who didn't understand who she was in Christ or that Jesus wanted to be the lover of her soul. He also saw a woman who failed to understand what high and holy callings marriage and motherhood are. Not long before this season of our lives, I had given up a challenging career in an office where I had received a lot of kudos on a regular basis, so staying at home with two kids was a hard adjustment for me. No one clapped when I scrubbed baby food off the highchair. No one cheered as I carted kids to ballet lessons and playgrounds. Greg recognized that I had looked to outside relationships for a sense of affirmation and as a remedy to the monotony of being a full-time, stay-at-home mom. 📖

11. Which, if any, of Shannon's feelings in her early years of marriage do you sympathize with? Have you also been tempted to seek affirmation outside of your roles as a mother and/or wife? Why or why not?

12. If your husband looked into your heart the way Greg was able to see into Shannon's, what would he see that probably no one else could?

13. Do you feel that things deep within your heart may be driving your current attitudes and behaviors? If so, how do those things drive you? If not, how have you safeguarded yourself from letting your innermost wounds and struggles drive you toward destructive relational patterns?

🌾 HARVESTING JOY AND PASSION
(Applying the Truth)

📖 Because Greg didn't run when I was honest with him about my struggles, I recognized what a trustworthy man I had married, and I felt safe and secure in a relationship for the first time in my life. I learned to appreciate his patience, his wisdom, and his spiritual maturity in not blaming himself for my emotional infidelity. Because of his help, I was able to establish my footing upon a firmer foundation.

Discovering Greg's deep level of commitment to me has been far more satisfying than any "intense" moment I've experienced with him or any other guy. I have his unconditional love—in spite of my flaws. This is what genuine intimacy is all about. And that intimacy is far better than butterflies, sweaty palms, fireworks, or any other form of intensity. 📖

14. Do you feel that you can be honest with your husband about your personal struggles? Do you feel he loves you unconditionally in spite of those struggles? Why or why not?

15. Do you feel that your husband can be honest with you about his personal struggles? Can you love him unconditionally in spite of those struggles? Why or why not?

📖 Of course, intimacy doesn't just happen automatically. It takes a tremendous amount of time and effort. Our relationships only grow and blossom when we nurture them, feed them, and intentionally care for them with diligence. Greg and I have achieved this level of intimacy only as a result of many counseling sessions and many hours spent in painful, honest conversation and gut-wrenching prayer. I've often thought that our intimate relationship has required a lot of blood, sweat, and tears—Jesus's blood, Greg's sweat, and my tears. But the fragrant beauty of what the three of us have created during those tumultuous years was well worth every ounce of effort. 📖

16. What issues have the two of you sweated or shed tears over? How has God responded to your efforts and/or to the cries of your hearts to improve your relationship?

17. In what practical ways have the two of you attempted to cultivate intimacy in your marriage? Describe these attempts.

18. Is cultivating a more intimate relationship a bigger challenge than you previously imagined? Why or why not?

📖 Greg often serves as a full-length mirror in my life by pointing out the embarrassing spiritual "spinach in my teeth," such as impatience, pride, greed, and selfishness—things I don't always notice about myself until I recognize that *he* notices them. When my husband gently brings these issues to my attention, our marriage can feel like a refiner's fire. These issues create incredible spiritual heat and bring my impurities to the surface and into plain sight. When this happens, I can stubbornly refuse to address these issues, pretending they are not really there, or I can humbly ask God to help me skim these impurities out of my life so that I am refined and can more accurately reflect Christ's perfection.

While we all hate to see the ugliness in our own lives, sanctification sessions can show us how we can grow spiritually and deepen our levels of personal holiness. When we strive toward more Christlike behavior, we are in essence saying to our spouses and to God, "You deserve better, so I'm going to try harder." Such an attitude honors both our spouses and God. 📖

19. Do you sense that your husband notices the spiritual "spinach in your teeth" more readily than the other people in your life? Why or why not?

20. Have you ever had thoughts that your husband deserves a "better" wife than you? If so, how did that thought make you feel?

21. Have you allowed feelings of insecurity or inadequacy drive you crazy, or do you allow them to drive you toward healthier choices and more mature behavior? How can you avoid the former and attempt the latter?

📖 Sure, it's disheartening when our spouses disappoint us. It can be frustrating when they don't live up to our expectations. It can be shocking when we discover that they have dark sides that we were unaware of. On the flip side, it's also humiliating to confess that we have major character flaws or that we struggle with sinful issues of our own or that we fail to live up to certain expectations that our spouses have of us. But in these times we each have a choice to make—we can choose to make things *bitter* with resentment and condemnation, or we can choose to make things *better* by displaying God's character traits of unconditional love and acceptance. 📖

22. What has been one of the most disheartening discoveries about your husband? How has he, at times, failed to live up to your expectations?

23. How can you keep a root of bitterness from developing in your heart over these issues? How can you make things better for him and for the two of you as a couple?

📖 Many people pray, "Lord, give me a ministry! Show me what I can do for you!" while the answer is right there under their noses. Yes, the world needs Jesus, but our spouses and children desperately need to be the primary recipients of our ministry efforts. If we save the world but lose our marriage or family in the process, what does that do to our witness? Can we really do more for others than we can do for those living under our same roof? As husbands and wives, fathers and mothers, we hold the power to minister to our own families in ways that no one else can. 📖

24. Have you failed to recognize the ministry opportunities that you have with the man sharing your bed every night? If so, how?

25. How have you effectively ministered to your husband in the past?

26. What do you sense he may need most from you during this season of his life? Are you willing to make him your primary ministry focus? Why or why not?

❧ GROWING TOGETHER
(Sharing the Truth in Small-Group Discussion)

> 📖 Because I had sought to remain in that "revved-up state of passionate love" with my husband, I failed to recognize the pleasure of our slowly developing "companionate love." Rather than beginning the hard work of stirring the embers of our relationship to renew a sense of excitement, I almost threw enough dirt on the fire to extinguish it altogether. Because I craved the euphoric happiness and intensity that are characteristic of a new relationship, I found myself gravitating toward new men—men who made me feel special, cherished, and desirable again because of the attention they gave me.
>
> Almost everywhere I went, I would meet a man who seemed to create in me that spark of excitement that Greg didn't seem to ignite anymore. My aerobics instructor made me feel sexy again as he complimented me on how great I was looking as I lost my extra pregnancy pounds. After years of staying at home and watching too many reruns of *Sesame Street* and *Barney*, my college professor reminded me of my intelligence when he praised my research papers or class participation. A friend at church made me feel like

a special confidante when he frequently called me at home during the day to complain about his marriage and to comment on how he wished his wife were more like me. I was getting lots of ego strokes, but they were all from superficial relationships—from men who only knew me from a distance. Greg, on the other hand, saw me close up. He knew the *real* me. 📖

27. Have you ever found yourself longing for those "revved-up states of passionate love"? What do you think is missing? Describe how this makes you feel and what effects it has on your contentment. If you don't long for these "revved-up states," explain how you've kept yourself grounded with more realistic expectations in your marriage.

28. How can a woman guard her heart and mind against extramarital pitfalls?

29. Rather than expecting "revved-up states of passionate love" to remain steady for decades, describe what a more mature "companionate love" might look like between you and your husband. What do you enjoy most about his companionship?

📖 I struggled during those years of my marriage because, like many women, I had failed to understand the difference between *intensity* and *intimacy*. *Intensity* is a feeling of extreme excitement or euphoria. It is a natural by-product of a brand-spanking-new relationship. Intensity often masquerades as intimacy. When we are getting to know new things about a person, we often think we are experiencing intimacy, but discovering new things about a stranger isn't intimate—it's just new. It may be exciting. It may feel intense. But it's often superficial and temporary. At best it's incomplete. For the most part, I only got to know the sides of these men that they wanted me to see. Those relationships often *felt* intimate, but the intimacy I was feeling was a false intimacy.

Genuine intimacy could only be found at home, where Greg and I both saw not just the good but also the bad and the ugly in each other. You see, *intimacy* can best be understood by breaking the word down into syllables: in-to-me-see. It's the ability to see into the heart, mind, and spirit of another person, which is impossible until after you've gotten to know that individual over a long period of time. It comes only after the intensity has worn off and you get to know things that most people can't possibly know unless they live with that person. 📖

30. Have you ever mistaken intensity for intimacy in a relationship? What do you recognize as the differences between the two?

31. Take what you have learned in this section of *Every Woman's Marriage* (the book) and write a more accurate description of intimacy in marriage.

32. If a wife pursued genuine intimacy rather than intensity in her marriage, what effects might it have on her husband? herself? their relationship?

📖 Time is a precious commodity that few of us have to spare. In these days of dual careers and overcommitted moms, it's no surprise that busyness is one of the biggest intimacy killers. The health complaints of busy women have actually led the medical community to coin a new term called the Hurried Woman Syndrome. Someone suffering from this syndrome may experience weight gain, low sex drive, moodiness, and fatigue. Doctors believe these symptoms are caused by the stress of doing too much, spreading oneself too thin, feeling overwhelmed and underaccomplished, and growing resentful of others' expectations, all of which can ultimately lead to hostility and depression.* 📖

33. Have you ever suffered any of the symptoms of Hurried Woman Syndrome? If so, what were they and what do you believe was causing them?

34. What are the things that commonly rob you of time and energy?

---

* Dr. Laura Schlessinger, *The Proper Care and Feeding of Husbands* (New York: HarperCollins, 2004), 21.

35. How can you redirect some of that time and energy toward enhancing your relationship with your husband? Is this a desire you have? Why or why not?

    📖 Imagine all the important relationships in your life and how long you get to enjoy each of them. Only one will remain consistent throughout your life—your relationship with your spouse. Decades of living under the same roof, sleeping in the same bed, eating at the same table, and sharing a rich emotional, mental, spiritual, and physical history together places this relationship in a class all by itself. Surely, the more you invest in your marriage, the greater the return on your investment. 📖

36. Based on what you currently invest in your marriage relationship, what will be the return five, ten, twenty, or even fifty years from now?

37. Are you willing you to invest more in your relationship in the present to yield a higher return in the future? If so, what would investing more look like for you?

⚬⚬

Dear Lord, help us to see the big picture and recognize the incredible treasure You've given us in marriage. We confess that we've perhaps not invested in our relationships as we should. Help us to embrace the companionate love we share with our husbands, to submit to the sanctification process that often accompanies marriage, and to make our husbands one of the primary recipients of our ministry efforts. Thank You for the opportunity to love them, to be loved by them, and to grow together in our love for You. Amen.

how his flame dies (part A)

Read chapters 6 and 7 in *Every Woman's Marriage.*

 PLANTING GOOD SEEDS
(Personally Seeking God's Truth)

As you seek to understand how your husband's flame of joy and passion for you might die, plant these good seeds in your heart:

> So now I am giving you a new commandment: Love each other. Just as I have loved you, you should love each other. Your love for one another will prove to the world that you are my disciples. (John 13:34–35)

> Don't just pretend that you love others. Really love them. Hate what is wrong. Stand on the side of the good. Love each other with genuine affection, and take delight in honoring each other. (Romans 12:9–10)

1. According to these verses, why is loving one another so important? What should love look like?

2. How can we apply these verses to marriage? How can we "love each other with genuine affection, and take delight in honoring each other" in marriage?

As you seek to understand what Christian love in marriage should look like, plant this seed in your heart:

> Love is patient and kind. Love is not jealous or boastful or proud or rude. Love does not demand its own way. Love is not irritable, and it keeps no record of when it has been wronged. It is never glad about injustice but rejoices whenever the truth wins out. Love never gives up, never loses faith, is always hopeful, and endures through every circumstance. (1 Corinthians 13:4–7)

3. Is the kind of love that Paul talks of in this passage truly attainable within marriage? Why or why not?

4. What three practical things could you do this week to be more patient, loving, and kind toward your husband?

⚒ WEEDING OUT DECEPTION
(Recognizing the Truth)

    📖 There have certainly been times when I fell into the mother role with Greg and expected him to simply obey me. I've insisted he be home from work at a certain time rather than trust that he'll come home as soon as he can. I've attempted to control what he eats and how often he exercises, as if he's clueless about living a healthy lifestyle on his own. I've created honey-do lists a mile long with the dates that I needed these things done by, as if his free time were completely mine to control…. Greg didn't appreciate it that his wife was trying to micromanage his life. 📖

5. Regardless of whether it's been your intention or not, would your husband say that you've ever tried to micromanage his life? Why or why not?

6. Have you ever felt as if someone was trying to control or manipulate you as though you were a child who had to submit to that person's authority? Describe how it made you feel or how you would imagine it to feel.

7. What are the biggest differences between the roles of a mother in a man's life and that of his wife? List as many as you can think of.

8. Describe some practical ways you can try to ensure your husband never feels as if you are trying to play the role of his mother rather than that of his wife.

📖 Although we may not have gotten *everything* we wanted when we were growing up, some girls were able to wrap their dads so tightly around their little fingers that they could bat their eyelashes and get pretty much whatever they wanted. That may be fine for a little girl, but when a woman emotionally manipulates her husband to get her way, she creates an unhealthy dynamic.

I felt sorry for one woman's husband when she told me, "I can get anything I want from Dan, within reason, of course. All I have to do is cross my legs and stop cooking, and he'll cave in after a couple of days." Translation: "I'll withhold sex and starve him until he caters to my every whim." 📖

9. Do you think it is wise for a woman to withhold sex, cooking, and so on, in an effort to manipulate her husband into doing what she wants? Why or why not?

10. Have there been times when you wanted your husband to cater to your whims or to give you what you desired most, regardless of his ability (or desire) to provide it for you? If so, describe one of these times and how it made each of you feel.

11. Describe a more effective approach that you can utilize whenever you desire your husband to do or provide something for you. What makes it more effective than manipulation?

> 📖 While I certainly don't want to minimize any woman's pain if she is living with an avowed nonbeliever, I do want to point out that legalism and self-righteousness are two things that Jesus spoke against more often than any other issue. Many of us have to admit that we often assign the bad guy role to our husbands while we wear the angelic halos. But what are we trying to accomplish when we do this? To guilt him into a more righteous lifestyle? Or to make ourselves look all the more holy by calling attention to his unholiness?
>
> Every Christian woman longs for a husband who is a strong spiritual leader in their home. But sometimes it takes years for a man to mature into such a role. Unfortunately, many women stunt that growth process with their own self-righteous indignation. 📖

12. Have there been times when you wanted your husband to be a stronger spiritual leader in your family? If so, how have you approached this situation and what's been the outcome?

13. What's a more effective approach to encouraging your husband to establish a personal relationship with Christ or to become more of a spiritual leader at home? Describe what this approach looks like.

📖 Satan can take something as tiny as a sigh, blow it way out of proportion in a person's mind, and cause a huge downward spiral in the relationship as a result. Something is said, and the hearer takes it out of context. The speaker is maybe just having a bad day, or is tired, or is feeling stressed because of something happening in the background of life. We are tempted to take it personally, and rather than keeping a short account of offenses, we build a case in our minds to prove that the person really doesn't love us, or respect us, or like us, or appreciate us, or want to be around us. With every negative incident that we let add up in our minds, we stack another brick between ourselves and that person, creating mental walls that only serve to separate us. But it doesn't have to be that way. 📖

14. Can you remember a time when you took a small incident and blew it way out of proportion, choosing to ride an emotional escalator rather than assuming the best about your husband? If so, what are your reflections about that experience?

15. Have you built any mental walls between you and your husband? If so, what can you do to remove the bricks and bring down that wall?

🐚 HARVESTING JOY AND PASSION
(Applying the Truth)

📖 Women frequently tell me, "I feel more like my husband's mother or boss than his partner," and that they are always harping

on their husbands about helping more around the house. If this
sounds familiar, remember that you can't *require* your husband's
cooperation. You can, however, *inspire* it. Because you want your
husband to be internally (rather than externally) motivated to help
out, try encouraging him with a nice comment, such as, "Would
you mind running the vacuum cleaner for me sometime today?
And when you do, remember how much I appreciate how hard
you work both inside and outside our home." Or when you see
him doing a particular chore, you might say, "I am so thankful to
have a guy who is willing to do that!" He'll feel like he's your hero
rather than your rebellious child, and chances are he'll be more
likely to want to play that heroic role more often in the future. 📖

16. In what ways do you make your husband feel like a hero? What compli-
ments or appreciative comments have you given him lately?

17. What does it mean to be *internally* motivated rather than *externally*
motivated? Which do you prefer? Which do you think your husband
would prefer?

18. How can you *inspire* his help rather than *require* it?

📖 Men are problem solvers by nature. They love to be our heroes, remedy our predicaments, and rescue us from our distresses. But when our problems are incredibly complex and deeply rooted, our husbands can feel overwhelmed and frustrated by their inability to fix things. So if you need a problem solved and your husband can solve it, feel free to look to him. But if you need therapy to overcome an ongoing issue that your husband isn't trained to handle, do yourself and your husband a favor and go to a therapist.

Of course, the reverse is also true. If your husband has deep-seated issues he needs to work through, it's unrealistic to expect that you are all the counselor he needs. Encourage and support him, but don't try to fix him on your own. You're his wife, not his therapist. 📖

19. What effect could it have on her marriage if a wife worked through her insecurities and hurts with a professional counselor rather than looking to her husband to "fix" her?

20. Do you have any issues that you think you (or your husband) may need to work through with the help of a counselor? If so, what keeps either of you from seeking that professional help? What good things could result in your marriage if you were to get help?

📖 But one particularly hectic morning of trying to get everyone up, dressed, fed, packed, and out the door for school and work, I let Greg's poor sense of direction put me on a high-speed emotional escalator. We pulled out of our driveway and stopped at a four-way intersection. Greg, as if on automatic pilot, turned left to go toward his office, even though we were en route to the kids' school, which required a right-hand turn. My tension had already been building all morning, and this was the little push that sent me right over the edge. I slammed my foot onto the imaginary brake pedal on the passenger floorboard and yelled, "*Where* are you going? Would you get your head out of the clouds and *pay attention,* for crying out loud?" As soon as the words came out of my mouth, I was flabbergasted by my own behavior, especially since my outburst had been in front of our kids.

Another one of Greg's quirks, which I've actually come to appreciate (much more than his poor sense of direction), is his inability to get riled up. Rather than yelling right back after my outburst at that four-way intersection or sarcastically asking if I wanted to do the driving instead, Greg looked calmly at me and said, "Could you have a little more patience with me? I wasn't thinking, but that doesn't give you the right to yell at me." Of course, he wasn't calm on the inside. He admits his heart felt incredibly hardened toward me in that moment. I had already eaten breakfast, but the situation called for a big helping of humble pie for dessert....

Now, instead of yelling at Greg, I put my hand on his thigh to get his attention, give him a cute little grin and an eyebrow raise, and ask, "Where are you going?" This approach enables him to laugh at himself with me. Even if we're running short on time, I tell myself, *What difference is it going to make to anyone's salvation if we're a couple of minutes late because Greg accidentally took a wrong turn?* 📖

21. Does your husband have any quirks that drive you crazy? If so, how might you respond to them so as not to hinder his flame of joy and passion for you?

❧ GROWING TOGETHER
(Sharing the Truth in Small-Group Discussion)

📖 Put a stop to playing games to get your needs or desires met. Granted, we all have times when we feel the need to nurture others, when we want to be nurtured by someone else, when we desire to help someone become a better person, or when we need to overcome issues to become better people ourselves, but game playing is never the answer. With God's help you can learn to recognize and verbalize those needs and desires such that your husband feels respected by you rather than manipulated.

The only way that you will ever truly experience relational fulfillment is by simply loving your husband for who God made him to be (rather than trying to make him play the role you want him to play). By recognizing and verbalizing your own needs or desires, you'll be setting the stage for *both* of you to feel like winners. 📖

22. Put a star beside the following mind games that you have played with your husband, and describe what you do when you play this game.

The Mommy-Child Game
The Spoiled Child–Sugar Daddy Game
The Holy Spirit–Wretched Sinner Game
The Patient-Psychotherapist Game
Other Mind Games

23. What unmet needs do you think you are experiencing when you play such games? How might you inspire—rather than demand—your husband to meet those needs?

    📖 Because I accepted his no, my husband wanted to give me a wholehearted yes whenever possible. I suspect that your husband is probably a lot like mine. When you pout, cry, or pitch a royal fit, it only makes him want all the more to dig his heels in the dirt. But if you take his no for an answer and respect his feelings, you will motivate your husband to consider seeing things from your perspective. I offer this not as a way for you to manipulate your husband more effectively but as a way to maintain unity and harmony, fueling the joy and passion you both desire and inspiring a more cooperative spirit in each of you. 📖

24. Have you ever failed to take your husband's no for an answer in order to get your way? If so, describe how he responded.

25. If you could rewind the tape and do things over again, what would you do differently to maintain unity in the relationship? Do you think it would have made a difference in your husband's response? Why or why not?

    📖 Try to refrain from having any expectations about what his answer *should* be when you ask what he's thinking. If you expect that he should be thinking about you and this is your reason for asking, you are fishing for affirmation or a compliment. But when you ask with pure motives (simply wanting to feel a connection with him in a given moment), you'll be able to accept any answer he gives, regardless of whether it's what you hoped to hear....

    Don't take it personally if his words don't match up to the imaginary script you dream of in your own mind. Let him connect with you in his own words and in his own special way. 📖

26. Do you at times fish for affirmation or a compliment from your husband, then feel disappointed because you don't hear what you'd hoped to hear?

27. Do you think it would be fair for your husband to feel disappointed if he asked you a question and you didn't tell him exactly what he wanted to hear?

28. How can you guard against creating expectations in your mind that your husband can't possibly fulfill?

29. God is the only One we can always depend on for the affirmation we crave. How, practically speaking, can you turn to Him to satisfy the longings of your heart?

    📖 Consider how it might impact your marriage for the better if you simply refused to take a small incident, blow it way out of proportion in your mind, and get overly emotional about it. What if you never sweated the small stuff and instead rolled with whatever unexpected punches life throws your way? What if you learned to laugh about your husband's poor sense of direction (or whatever little personality quirk he has that can drive you insane with frustration)? What if you could accept his no without any manipulative drama? What if you learned to give your husband the grace to have his own thoughts and you refused to take things personally? What if you held firmly to the belief that your husband loves you like crazy and desires to be intimate with you whenever possible? Wouldn't it be much easier to ignite and maintain incredible joy and passion in your relationship?

    You bet it would. So do yourself (and your husband) a favor and try to remain grounded whenever you sense the temptation to take another emotional escalator ride. 📖

30. Why do you think some women are prone to emotional escalation? Is this true of you? If so, in what way?

31. As you look at the things you've complained about in your marriage, ask yourself if they are important enough to warrant disrupting the harmony in your relationship. Why or why not?

32. How can you keep the main thing (joy and passion) as the main thing and not sweat the small stuff that can wreak havoc in your marriage?

∞

*L*ord *Jesus, from the beginning of time, women have played manip-ulative mind games to get their ways or justify their bad behaviors. We deeply desire to be amazing women who exemplify Christ in our marriages and in this world, yet we often behave in ways that aren't in line with this desire. Show us what kind of mind games we fall prey to and what kind of emotional escalators we hop on, so we can avoid the dysfunctional dynamics they create in our marriages. Teach us to recognize our own needs and to communicate them to our loved ones in ways that inspire them to help meet those needs. In Your most holy and precious name, amen.*

how his flame dies (part B)

Read chapters 8 and 9 of *Every Woman's Marriage.*

🌱 PLANTING GOOD SEEDS
(Personally Seeking God's Truth)

As you seek to avoid unhealthy comparisons, plant this good seed in your heart:

> We do not dare to classify or compare ourselves with some who
> commend themselves. When they measure themselves by them-
> selves and compare themselves with themselves, they are not wise.
> (2 Corinthians 10:12, NIV)

1. Why do we compare ourselves to other people? Why do we compare
   our husbands to other men?

2. How can you guard your heart against unhealthy comparisons? What
   thought can you meditate on when you catch your mind drifting in this
   direction?

As you consider how you may encourage your husband in his on- and off-the-clock pursuits, plant these good seeds in your heart:

> But encourage one another daily, as long as it is called Today, so that none of you may be hardened by sin's deceitfulness. (Hebrews 3:13, NIV)

> And let us consider how we may spur one another on toward love and good deeds. (Hebrews 10:24, NIV)

> Therefore encourage one another and build each other up, just as in fact you are doing. Now we ask you, [sisters], to respect those who work hard among you, who are over you in the Lord and who admonish you. (1 Thessalonians 5:11–12, NIV)

3. Can you remember a specific time when someone did something that encouraged you? What did that person do? How did it make you feel?

4. How can you be more of an encouragement to your husband? How do you think he would feel if you began doing and saying things every day to encourage him?

🔖 WEEDING OUT DECEPTION
(Recognizing the Truth)

> 📖 What about you? Are you ever resentful of your husband's job? jealous of things he gets to do? adamant that he change or not change careers because of how it may affect you?

I realize that there are situations when a wife needs to gently speak up, especially if her husband is a workaholic or regularly ignores the needs of his family. But if you are like me, there are times when your dissatisfaction is born out of selfishness or of jealousy of the time and energy your husband pours into his career, because it takes him away from you. 📖

5. Do you ever compare your career or lifestyle to your husband's and feel envious of the time and attention he pours into his professional pursuits? Do you ever feel as if you play second fiddle to his job? Why or why not?

6. Do you think your husband would want you to feel the way you do about the time and energy he invests in his job or career? Why or why not?

7. Are you able to express appreciation for how hard your husband works outside and/or inside the home? Why or why not? What steps can you take to show him how you feel?

📖 I began staying home and letting Greg go to his games by himself more and more, even though he urged me to come each time.
I thought I was making a point by refusing to go, but after a while,
I dreaded the sound of the door closing and the car driving off
while I stayed at home with two kids. I didn't like him going to
games because I wanted him to stay home with me, and I made
sure he knew that before he left. I felt as if softball was a much
higher priority to Greg than our family was, and I felt cheated. I
came to see softball as a mistress that he was more faithful to than
he was to me. I couldn't recognize that softball was the outlet my
husband desperately needed to recharge his physical, mental, and
emotional batteries. 📖

8. Does your husband have a sport or hobby that takes a significant
   amount of time or takes his focus away from you? If so, how have
   you felt about it and why?

9. Have you ever felt you should be allowed time off to shop, do things
   with your girlfriends, or pursue a hobby, yet resented it when your husband expressed a similar expectation? After reading this section, have
   your feelings about his off-the-clock activities changed at all? If so, how?
   If not, why?

📖 One of the most shameful mistakes I've ever made was once
saying to Greg early in our marriage, "You just don't seem to
approach me with as much whirlwind passion as I'm used to. If

you could be a little more enthusiastic in sweeping me off my feet and into bed, I'd be more willing to go there."

He responded kindly but firmly, "Shannon, don't ever compare me to another man that you had no business being in a sexual relationship with in the first place."

It was another *Ouch!* moment in the life of Shannon Ethridge but a much needed wake-up call, pointing out that I had been unfairly comparing Greg to a past lover. If the tables had been turned and Greg had said something along the lines of, "You know, you aren't as thin or beautiful as some of the other girls I've been attracted to. If you would lose a few pounds and fix yourself up a little more, I'd be much more attentive," I would have been cut to the core. I'm sure that in that moment, he must have felt the same way. 📖

10. Have you given in to the temptation of comparing your husband to your boss? coworker? father? pastor? friend? another man? If so, who is that person and what about him do you admire or wish your husband could emulate?

11. Now list five things that your husband does well or that you love about him.

📖 Most of us have someone in our lives who drives us to unhealthy comparisons, whether it's the perky personal trainer at the fitness club, the happy little homemaker next door who has all her photos in a Creative Memories scrapbook and cuts her kids' sandwiches in the shape of stars, or the sexy glamour queens who grace the silver screen....

It's easy to compare ourselves to other women and to ruminate on all the ways that we don't measure up.... When we do this, we rob ourselves of our peace, our joy, and our confidence. We also put our husbands in an incredibly tight spot as we fish for the affirmation we need with such questions as "Am I as pretty as she is? as good a cook? as good a housekeeper?" Most men are smart enough to know that the answer to any such question should always be "Of course, dear!" so don't bother asking your husband. It only magnifies your own insecurities in both your eyes and his. It also places the burden of responsibility on his shoulders to make you feel good about yourself, but feeling good about yourself is a gift that only *you* can give *yourself.* 📖

12. To whom have you compared yourself in the past, only to feel discouraged because that individual outshines you somehow? What did you admire about this person?

13. How can you affirm that person for that particular gift, talent, or attribute without coveting it for yourself? Can you be genuinely happy for that person rather than envious? Why or why not?

14. Do you feel good about who you are—what you look like, how you interact with others, and so on? If so, list five things you like about yourself. If not, list why you don't feel good about yourself and consider seeing a counselor about those issues.

🌾 HARVESTING JOY AND PASSION
(Applying the Truth)

> 📖 While women often have a mind-boggling number of responsibilities to tend to, we can't forget that our husbands also face a whirlwind of challenges every day. Not only do they need to bring home the bacon, they need to make enough money to save for the future. Not only do they need to get the job done, they need to impress the boss and coworkers and meet quotas and deadlines in a way that shows they are capable, decisive, and efficient.
>
> Your husband faces a plethora of daily pressures, and every hour of his day can sometimes feel like an uphill battle. He needs to know, beyond a shadow of a doubt, that someone is on his side, regardless of how well or how poorly he feels he's doing that day. He needs someone who is committed to rooting him on to success both at work and at home. 📖

15. List the ways in which your husband contributes to your marriage, kids, and household (for example, he goes to work every day to bring home money, plays soccer with the kids, handles the bills, maintains the cars, helps with dishes, gives me a few minutes to myself).

16. Now list some ways you can show your husband how much you appreciate his contributions (for example, make his favorite dessert, detail his car, tuck a note in his lunch, plan a getaway date together). Once you've made your list, circle at least one and carry it out this week.

📖 Greg has often felt caught between my conflicting desires. From one side of my mouth I'm telling him I want him to spend more time with our family, and from the other I'm telling him that I want a better standard of living....

Remember, most men don't need a lot of stuff in order to be happy. Greg was perfectly happy in a next-to-naked apartment for two years before we got married. While I've learned to decorate on a tight budget, the most important lesson I've learned is that genuine happiness doesn't come from having nicer stuff or a bigger house. Happiness is found in the love we have for one another and the memories we make together as a family. 📖

17. Do you ever want things you can't have or afford? How does it make you feel?

18. How do you think it makes your husband feel when he knows you want something he can't provide?

19. Identify some of your favorite childhood memories or some special moments you've shared with your husband and kids. Why do you remember those times so fondly? Was money or stuff part of the reason?

20. What thing(s) spoke to you most in chapter 9, "Comparing Apples and Oranges"?

21. What impact would it have on your marriage and family if you learned to be content with your husband, yourself, and your possessions? How can you become more content with what you *do* have?

❧ Growing Together
(Sharing the Truth in Small-Group Discussion)

📖 If your husband were unemployed and you had no salary to live on, would his current situation be a welcome change in your wondering how your family would keep a roof over its head and food in the pantry? I don't mean to be melodramatic, but let's put things into perspective. The next time you feel resentful of your husband's career, ask yourself if you have a legitimate complaint and if adjustments can be made. If so, discuss your concerns calmly and respectfully. For example, you might start off with, "Honey, can we sit down and assess how our lives are going right now and talk about what's most important to each of us and to our family?" If you realize that adjustments can't be made for whatever reason, know that your husband needs your encouraging support far more than he needs your resentment. Do what you can to let him know that you are his biggest fan and that you want him to succeed at work and to feel good about his ability to provide for his family. That's the kind of cheerleader he's going to want to come home to whenever possible. 📖

22. Tell the group about some of the things you've done or said to encourage your husband in his roles as a husband, father, and employer or employee. How did he respond? How did his response make you feel?

23. Also share some of the ideas you wrote down (in question 16) for how you would like to express appreciation toward your husband in the future. Ask the group to hold you accountable for doing the thing you circled by the next meeting.

📖 Over the next several years, Greg was a teetotaler, not playing or watching any sports out of submission to my desires. But he was also dying on the vine. Without the relief outlet he'd found in softball, he was more stressed about his work and less excited about life. At the time I didn't connect the change in Greg to his withdrawal from sports. But if I had been more committed to seeing

Greg's heart and to meeting his needs, I would have seen that even though I had succeeded in getting him to spend more time with our family, I had belittled him for his love of sports and made him feel guilty. I may as well have literally ripped out his heart and stomped on it....

Perhaps your husband doesn't have a passion for sports but rather some other activity that gives him a sense of joy and satisfaction. Perhaps he retreats to the outdoors to hunt, fish, or dig around in the garden, or immerses himself in a new computer software program, or hides out in the basement with his guitar or other musical instrument. Whatever your husband's hobby, I encourage you not to take his passion for it personally. Don't be his opponent by assuming that he uses these hobbies as an escape from his family (which is more than likely not true). Instead, encourage him to do the things he loves and is energized by. When we allow our husbands this time, we inspire them to return to us as much happier campers, with greater desires to connect emotionally with us. 📖

24. What does your husband love to do in his free time that really energizes him? How do you feel about this hobby or activity? Why?

25. What if your husband told you, "Honey, why don't you take the whole day to do whatever you love doing? I'll take care of the kids and the house. You go shopping or read a novel in front of the fireplace all day." How would you feel?

26. Now what if you told your husband, "Honey, why don't you take next
    Saturday to do whatever you want to do that you've not gotten to do in
    a while? Feel free to spend all day on the golf course or tinkering in your
    shop." How do you think he would feel? Can you imagine making such
    a gesture? Why or why not?

      Unfortunately, I'm not the only wife who has fallen into the
   trap of comparing her husband to other men. Consider these comments and ask yourself if you have ever alluded to such a sentiment
   in any way:
   - "Her husband still takes her out on a date each week and
     sends her cards and flowers often. How come you don't do
     that for me anymore?"
   - "Why can't you be as handy around the house as my dad?
     He would have had that problem fixed in no time!"
   - "It really makes me feel special when the guys at the office
     will take a few moments just to talk to me and ask how my
     day is going. Why can't you show such an interest?"
   - "He must really love his wife the way he takes such good care
     of their yard. How do you think the way our yard looks
     makes me feel?"

27. Have you ever been guilty of making such comparative statements to or
    about your husband? If so, was the comment you made appropriate in
    light of what you learned in this part of the book? Why or why not?

28. How can you avoid unhealthy comparisons and become more sensitive about your choice of words?

📖 Chances are, if you are reading this book, you do have a husband—something most single women would love to have. If you are able to get up and exercise, do so with a happy heart, thanking God for your good health. If you have children of your own, be grateful that you aren't one of the multitudes of women who struggle with infertility month after month. If you have a roof over your head, food in your pantry, and gas in your car, you are actually among the wealthiest people on the planet compared to those In many other countries.

The next time you are tempted to compare apples to oranges, or to compare your own situation to a seemingly better one, remember that God has custom-tailored these blessings especially for you, especially for this season of your life. He has given you a unique size, shape, and personality, all to be used for His glory rather than your own. He has given you a marvelously unique husband and perhaps children, complete with a few character flaws that serve as great reminders that no one is perfect in every way. He has blessed you with a comfortable home where you can take refuge from the world and make memories that will warm your heart more and more with each passing birthday.

Absolutely nothing can compare to the joy of finding contentment in these remarkable gifts that the Lord lavishes upon us. And displaying that joy is the secret to fanning your husband's flame for you. Just ask any husband whose wife has learned the art of contentment rather than the craft of comparison, and he'll more than likely tell you that he is one happy man. 📖

29. You probably remember the hymn, "Count Your Blessings." What three
things are you most grateful for in your life?

&

*Lord, we confess that we sometimes resent the time our husbands
spend at work and that we envy the woman next door who seems to
have her act together. Help us to be our husbands' biggest fans and
help them find confidence in the fact that their wives are their own
personal cheerleaders. Convict us when we look upon others' attrib-
utes, relationships, or possessions with jealousy rather than with genuine happiness. Remind us that in You we have everything we need,
and teach us how to be content with the multitude of blessings You
bestow on us. In Jesus's name, amen.*

from death to life again

Read chapters 10 and 11 of *Every Woman's Marriage.*

PLANTING GOOD SEEDS
(Personally Seeking God's Truth)

As you seek to understand what it means for couples to mutually submit, plant this seed in your heart:

> And further, you will submit to one another out of reverence for
> Christ. You wives will submit to your husbands as you do to the
> Lord. For a husband is the head of his wife as Christ is the head
> of his body, the church; he gave his life to be her Savior. As the
> church submits to Christ, so you wives must submit to your hus-
> bands in everything.
>
> And you husbands must love your wives with the same love
> Christ showed the church. (Ephesians 5:21–25)

1. Some women cringe when they hear the *s* word—*submission*. Why do
   women have such a negative response to this concept?

2. Why did Paul say we are to "submit to one another" in verse 21? Explain what you believe Paul meant.

3. What advice would you give a new bride who is struggling with the concept of mutual submission?

As you seek to give your husband what he really wants most (your smile!), plant these good seeds in your heart:

> Always be full of joy in the Lord. I say it again—rejoice! Let every-one see that you are considerate in all you do. Remember, the Lord is coming soon. (Philippians 4:4–5)

> We were filled with laughter,
>   and we sang for joy.
> And the other nations said,
>   "What amazing things the LORD has done
>   for them."
> Yes, the LORD has done amazing things for us!
>   What joy! (Psalm 126:2–3)

> The LORD is my strength, my shield from every danger.
>   I trust in him with all my heart.
> He helps me, and my heart is filled with joy.
>   I burst out in songs of thanksgiving.
>   (Psalm 28:7)

4. Are you able to choose to be joyful because of what God has done for you, even if your temporary circumstances may not warrant joy at the time? Why or why not?

✎ WEEDING OUT DECEPTION
(Recognizing the Truth)

📖 Our husbands aren't mind readers, and they may have their own ideas about how they prefer to accomplish various tasks. As long as things get done, do they really have to get done *our* way? Only if we want to make our husbands resent having to help us. 📖

5. Have you ever helped someone with a particular task, only to have that person dictate exactly how you were to do the job or criticize you for not doing it "right"? If so, how did you feel? Were you inspired to continue helping?

6. Is there a specific chore or task that you insist your husband do *your* way? How do you imagine it makes him feel when you fail to appreciate *his* way of doing it?

📖 What might be the reason you seek to win arguments every time or to get that last word in? Is it so you can feel superior? more

intelligent or articulate? Are you merely resorting to childish behavior because you've not learned to respond to strife like a mature
adult? Or do you try to inflict harm on your husband so that there's
some sense of justification or revenge for your own pain?

When we insist on getting the last word, we don't resolve any
disagreements. We only cement them in our husbands' minds as
they leave the room feeling disrespected and resentful. I'm sure
you'll agree with me: winning an argument isn't nearly as important
as ultimately winning your husband's admiration and affection. 📖

7. Is winning your husband's admiration and affection more important to
   you than winning an argument? Why or why not?

8. Can you recall a time you when you sought to win an argument, even
   at the expense of your husband's feelings? If so, how does it make you
   feel in hindsight?

9. Can you recall a time when you and your husband differed on something, yet you recognized that winning the argument wasn't the most
   important thing? If so, how did the disagreement end? How might it
   have ended if you had not handled the situation the way you did?

📖 Beware of ever playing the God card.... For many women this is simply a spiritualized form of control over our husbands. If such is the case, can you imagine how God might feel about us using His name to justify our attempts at controlling our husbands? In humility, we need to remember that our believing husbands can usually hear from God as easily as we can, and there's always a possibility that God may give our husbands a word that we've not yet received. 📖

10. Are there times when you feel you are more spiritually aware than your husband of what God expects? If so, what makes you feel this way? Do you think your feelings are justified? Why or why not?

11. In your own words, explain what "playing the God card" means. What do you suspect is behind this behavior?

12. Suppose you choose *not* to play the God card but rather trust that your husband can hear from God as easily as you can. How will this make your husband feel? Why?

📖 What's usually behind a woman's quest for control? Experts agree that an overwhelming need to control is actually an outward manifestation of the inward insecurities we feel. When we're good with ourselves, we're usually good with almost everyone around us. But when we're not feeling so good about ourselves, we often seek to assign the blame to someone outside of ourselves, ruminating on such thoughts as, *If my husband were more attentive... If my kids were better behaved... If my home were more in order... If my coworkers were more appreciative... Then my world would be a better place and I'd feel and act like a better person.*

Of course, controlling women will tell you that they *must* be controlling for anything to get done because their husbands are so passive. But it's worth asking ourselves, *Am I controlling because he's so passive, or is he passive because I'm so controlling?* 📖

13. Did this particular excerpt strike a chord in you? Have you found that when you don't feel good about yourself, you need to control others? Why or why not? Or do you have another theory as to what causes you to feel out of control at times? (Remember to focus on what's going on inside of you rather than on how others around you are behaving.)

14. What things can you do to exercise the best form of control— *self-control*—rather than attempting to control those around you?

🦞 HARVESTING JOY AND PASSION
(Applying the Truth)

📖 Consider the example of a chief executive officer and a chief operations officer. (For simplicity's sake, we'll refer to the CEO as "he" and the COO as "she.") Ultimately, the CEO is the leader in charge, but he delegates the authority to lead the day-to-day operations to the COO. The COO is free to set goals, direct the staff, make decisions and suggestions, offer feedback, and so on, but she does it as an *extension* of the CEO, not because she feels the CEO is incompetent or unwilling to do it himself. She constructively controls many areas of operation, but she always respects the fact that she's under the CEO's umbrella of authority. Her position isn't a threat to the CEO at all, but rather a benefit and a blessing.

Now apply this same relational dynamic to marriage. Ultimately, God has given husbands the charge of being the spiritual head of the household, but God also created woman as a "helpmate" to man. Think of woman as a COO of sorts who is under her husband's authority, the CEO of their family. She may be the one setting certain goals, calling many shots, directing the staff (or children), making decisions, and so on. But rather than doing so begrudgingly because her husband's not around all day or because she feels he's incapable of doing it himself, she operates in this role with excellence as an extension of him. She's under his authority, but she willingly receives the delegation of certain realms of responsibility as a vital part of his team. 📖

15. Do you see yourself as a capable chief operations officer under the authority of your husband? Or are you tempted at times to think that you have to run the show because your husband's not capable? Why do you feel the way you do?

16. Would your husband agree with your assessment? If he, as your chief executive officer, were asked to give you a periodic review, how would he rate your performance? your attitude? Why?

17. Identify three things you could do to develop a more positive attitude about the roles you play within your marriage, family, and home.

18. How would it impact your life if you exhibited a positive team player attitude? How would it affect your husband? your children?

    📖 Many women complain that their husbands don't initiate family devotions or prayer time together. So what's wrong with the wife acting as the COO and cheerfully *offering* to read a devotion or say a prayer, or respectfully *inviting* the CEO to do so? You may be amazed at how well received such an invitation, offered with the right attitude, may be. Remember, just because a wife thinks of the idea or initiates more often doesn't mean that she's the spiritual leader. It simply means she's a great helpmate. 📖

19. Have you held the opinion that for your husband to fulfill his role as the spiritual leader, he must initiate all the spiritual activity in your home? If so, what gave you this opinion?

20. How can you let go of any expectation that your husband should always be the spiritual initiator? How do you think this new perspective could affect your marriage and family?

📖 Your husband's greatest desire doesn't revolve around sex, sports, sandwiches, sitcoms, or success, but around putting a smile on your face. I've asked Greg to tell you why this is so—at least from one male's perspective: "A few years ago, Shannon asked what attracted me most to her while we were dating.... What attracted me most was that Shannon was happy whenever I was around (and relatively unhappy whenever we had to be apart). Her smile made me feel really great about myself and my ability to make a woman like her happy.... Everyone wants to be in the presence of someone who makes them feel good about *themselves*—it's just human nature.... A man's self-esteem is wrapped up in how good of a husband, father, provider, friend, and lover he is. When we're not making the grade and we see the disappointment on our wife's face as a result, it's like looking into a mirror and seeing the loser we've always feared becoming." 📖

21. How do you think your husband feels about himself when he looks at the expression you have on your face most of the time? Why?

22. If you were to make the conscious choice to smile more often, what effect might it have on your husband's self-esteem? Why?

    📖 You—more than anyone else—have the power to make your husband's day. You may find it helpful to sit down and make as long a list as possible of things you can be happy about. Even when I'm in the bluest of moods, I can always rattle off a long list of blessings that God has bestowed upon me, such as my salvation, my marriage, my children, good health, a loving extended family, great friends, ministry opportunities, healing for the past, security for today, hope for tomorrow, and so on.

    What about you? How long a list can you think of just off the top of your head? Enough to bless your husband with a smile and a warm look of contentment? 📖

23. Are there things in your life that you often forget to smile about? Go ahead—make a list of the blessings you can be happy about.

❦ **GROWING TOGETHER**
(Sharing the Truth in Small-Group Discussion)

24. What portion of this week's readings spoke to you, convicted you, or encouraged you most? Share that passage with others and explain why it meant so much to you.

📖 But why do we become so controlling when company is due to arrive? Because we want our guests to feel special, but I also believe it can be a pride thing. We want others to think we are a perfect family who lives in a perfect house. But the reality is, we all have occasional dust bunnies on the floor, toothpaste in the sink, or imprints on the bedspread. Maybe we should focus more effort on developing a hospitable frame of mind before company arrives instead of obsessing over every detail of our houses and every neglectful act of our husbands. 📖

25. Do you often suffer from "precompany perfection"? If so, why? If not, how do you avoid this relational pitfall?

📖 We are following in Eve's footsteps when we seek control rather than submissiveness. When we seek control, we sometimes *create* the exact behavior in our husbands that we abhor. I confess I've been guilty in the past of insisting that Greg do things my way, and then resenting him for not being a stronger leader in our home. I've dragged him into counseling for his "passivity issues" when, in fact, my control issues were ultimately the real root of our problems. When this dynamic is present, it's like what Jesus said in Mark 3:25, "If a house is divided against itself, that house cannot stand" (NIV). It creates a Catch-22 situation for both spouses. She wants him to lead, but she doesn't want to let go of the reins. He feels damned if he gives up control and damned if he doesn't. No one wins when spouses are in a power struggle. We can't complete each other as helpmates if we are competing with one another for control.

Therefore, when women ask, "How do I get my husband to take the wheel and be the leader?" I tell them, "By getting out of the driver's seat!" In most cases, as long as a wife is trying to manipulate and control, her husband will usually ride along in the backseat for the sake of unity and in an effort to keep her happy. But if a wife will trust her husband and follow him, even when she doesn't necessarily agree with how he's driving or where he's taking her, he might just develop the courage or the desire to become the leader that she wants him to be. 📖

26. If your marriage were a car, who would be in the driver's seat? Has your need for control ever been a source of tension in your relationship? Why or why not?

27. If you have a tendency to try to be in control in your marriage, how can you make a conscious effort to let go of the wheel?

28. What effect might surrendering the need for control have on your life? your marriage? your family?

    📖 Indeed, happiness is a choice, and being happy can simply be a matter of smiling more often. In fact, some studies indicate that our facial expressions are not so much a reflection of our feelings, but that our feelings are largely a reflection of the facial expression we wear.* I've experimented with this theory, and it works. The more I smile, the happier I feel. We are free to choose both our facial expressions and our attitudes in any given situation. 📖

29. Test this theory for a moment. Look around the room and smile at several people, or if you are by yourself, smile into a mirror for a minute or two. Do you feel different? How so?

30. What difference would it make in your household if your husband and children came home each day to a woman who had a smile on her face? Why? Is this a goal you'd like to strive for?

---

* Malcolm Gladwell, *Blink* (New York: Little, Brown and Company, 2005), 206.

∞

Lord, You've given us so much to smile about, yet we often fail to reflect Your joy, peace, and fulfillment on our faces. Turn our frowns upside down and help us radiate Your love to others simply by choosing to be happy. Especially help us in our quest to surrender prideful forms of control when we behave like Mrs. (Always) Right. Remind us to focus our energies on controlling ourselves, our tongues, and our attitudes rather than on trying to control others. Encourage our husbands to have the confidence to fulfill their leadership roles in our homes, and give us the grace to go along with them on this wonderful ride called marriage. Amen.

reigniting joy and passion

Read chapters 12, 13, and 14 of *Every Woman's Marriage*.

🌱 PLANTING GOOD SEEDS
(Personally Seeking God's Truth)

As you seek to respect your husband, plant this good seed in your heart:

> So again I say, each man must love his wife as he loves himself, and
> the wife must respect her husband. (Ephesians 5:33)

1. As mentioned in chapter 12 of *Every Woman's Marriage,* the Greek word
   Paul uses for "respect" is *phobeo,* which means "to be in awe of" or "to
   revere."* Do you consider your husband worthy of high regard? Does
   he inspire awe in you? How so?

---

* Shaunti Feldhahn, *For Women Only: What You Need to Know about the Inner Lives of Men*
(Sisters, OR: Multnomah, 2004), 27.

2. Do you make the choice to revere your husband? What do you do to express to him your reverence or respect?

As you seek to become a pleasant person to live with, plant these seeds in your heart:

> It is better to live alone in the corner of an attic than with a contentious wife in a lovely home. (Proverbs 21:9)

> It is better to live alone in the desert than with a crabby, complaining wife. (Proverbs 21:19)

3. Are there days when your testiness causes your husband to prefer to be in the corner of an attic or in the desert rather than be with you? If so, how can you turn your home from a place of strife to a place of sanctuary?

As you consider how you can become less irritable and more loving, plant this seed in your heart:

> If I could speak in any language in heaven or on earth but didn't love others, I would only be making meaningless noise like a loud gong or a clanging cymbal. If I had the gift of prophecy, and if I knew all the mysteries of the future and knew everything about everything, but didn't love others, what good would I be? And if I had the gift of faith so that I could speak to a mountain and make

it move, without love I would be no good to anybody. If I gave
everything I have to the poor and even sacrificed my body, I could
boast about it; but if I didn't love others, I would be of no value
whatsoever. (1 Corinthians 13:1–3)

4. Do the words "no value whatsoever" sound daunting to you? If so, what
   might you do to be more loving toward others so that you become more
   valuable to God's kingdom?

WEEDING OUT DECEPTION
(Recognizing the Truth)

📖 If you want to ignite your husband's joy and passion for you,
you'll carefully consider your words to ensure that they communicate acceptance and respect. Ask him to tell you what things you
say to him that cause him to feel disrespected—and then deter-
mine not to use those words again. Think about what respectful
words you could use in their place, and then do so.

When you choose your words wisely and demonstrate respect
for your husband, you'll reap many benefits. Not only will he
feel good because he knows he pleases you, but your children will
also grow to revere him all the more, and they will revere you as
well.... Your marriage relationship will be enhanced, and your
family will benefit from the security of a respectful atmosphere at
home. Most of all, you'll please God with your attempts to show
the respect that your husband, His beloved son, deserves—not
because he does everything perfectly to deserve such reverence,
but because he is divinely and uniquely created in his heavenly
Father's image. 📖

5. If the way your husband feels about himself were contingent upon how you treat him, how do you think he feels?

6. If you have children, how do they treat their father? Are they reflecting how you treat him? How so?

📖 Of course, conflict is inevitable in any close relationship. It's not a matter of *if,* but simply a matter of *when* disagreements arise. Conflict doesn't mean we have a bad relationship or that we are unhappily married. Conflicts are simply opportunities for couples to grow in understanding of each other and to work out amiable resolutions. However, *how* we handle the conflict does have a bearing on the ongoing quality of the intimacy we share. So, in those moments when we don't see eye to eye, it's important not to let our emotions get out of control....

Most men find emotional tantrums annoying and will dig their heels in deeper rather than be manipulated by screaming or unnecessary crying.

So keep your voice at a normal level, face your husband, maintain eye contact, and even hold hands or have some part of your bodies touching. This kind of body language is much more effective than a turned back, folded arms, or rolling eyes. Remember, actions speak louder than words. 📖

7. Think of the last time you and your husband had a disagreement. What kind of body language did you use? Do you believe your actions demonstrated respect or disrespect? Why?

8. What's the difference between being upset because you are genuinely hurt versus being upset so you can punish or manipulate? Are you usually able to express your emotions calmly, or do you overdramatize so you get your way?

 📖 In times of conflict, avoid taking the offensive or getting defensive and going head to head against each other. Remember that you are on the same team, fighting for victory over the opposing forces of anger, bitterness, unforgiveness, and so on.

 Sadly, most of us enter conflict with one main goal—to win! And we usually assume that for us to win, the other person has to *lose.* But if you are familiar at all with Stephen Covey's *Seven Habits of Highly Effective People,* you'll more than likely recall his success strategy to develop a win-win mentality. To think win-win rather than win-lose is not only more effective in business but also in personal relationships, especially marriage. The most favorable strategy to maintain joy and passion in the midst of conflict is to figure out what kind of compromise can be had so that you both walk away feeling like a winner. 📖

9. What is the biggest recurring argument in your marriage? Who's usually on the offensive and who's on the defensive? Why?

10. What if both of you sat down and calmly discussed possible win-win solutions? Do you think you could come to an agreement? What might that agreement look like? (Remember, he needs to walk away feeling like a winner too!)

🐚 HARVESTING JOY AND PASSION
(Applying the Truth)

📖 Intimacy is risky. As a husband and wife over time reveal to each other who they really are, they both hope that the other person will be unconditionally loving and accepting. If both spouses feel accepted and loved, then emotional, spiritual, and physical closeness usually results. But if one spouse feels unaccepted and unloved, that person will retreat, resulting in emotional, spiritual, and physical distance. To be free to open up and be ourselves in any relationship, we must first feel safe. If we feel unsafe, we will most likely withdraw into ourselves rather than risk trying to connect with the person who causes us to feel rejected in the first place. That's why acceptance is a key factor in building the kind of intimate marriage relationship we long for. 📖

11. If a stranger on the street approached your husband and asked, "Do you believe your wife accepts you for who you really are?" how do you think he would respond? Why?

12. If you long for a deeper level of intimacy with your husband, are you willing to go out of your way to demonstrate unconditional love and acceptance to inspire such intimacy? How might you do that more effectively?

📖 You also might want to talk with your husband about giving both of you permission to lovingly pull the other aside whenever one senses an attitude of rejection. Both of you need to feel the freedom to say, "My heart is beginning to feel closed toward you, and neither of us wants that. What's really going on here, and how can we get back on track?" or "I sense that your heart is growing cold toward me. Is there something that I've done or said that has caused you to feel this way? I really love you, and I want you to feel fully accepted, so help me treat you the way you deserve to be treated."

Greg and I have given each other permission to say these kinds of things to each other, and as a result we've been better able to keep short accounts with each other and to remain spiritually connected. 📖

13. Explain what you think it means to "keep short accounts with each other." Do you believe the two of you do this successfully? Why or why not?

14. If you were feeling hurt by your husband, wouldn't you want him to ask you what he had done to hurt you and how he could make the situation right? Do you think you could demonstrate the same concern to him the next time you sense him growing distant? Why or why not?

📖 If couples make time (notice I said *make* time, not *find* time) to connect with each other on a regular basis, we can actually prevent conflicts from forming, or at least prevent them from becoming any more of an issue than they really need to be....

Indeed, we don't grow close or remain connected simply by coexisting in the same house and sleeping in the same bed. Lasting love takes tremendous effort. Strong relationships require work. Conflict is bound to come, but it can actually make our marriages stronger if we choose our words carefully, express our emotions calmly, respect each other's feelings, and work toward compromise. 📖

15. Because we rarely find time, how can you and your husband make time to prevent conflicts from forming? What's the best time of the day or week for you to keep an appointment to simply connect with each other?

📖 You can't blame a guy for wanting his home to reflect a little of *his* personality and hobbies, wanting to have some territory in the house that *he* can control, and wanting to have the freedom to relax and not worry about keeping everything spotless at all times. Women want the same thing. We want to reflect our tastes in our décor, to arrange rooms to suit us, and to have at least some space where we can just close the door and not worry about it being presentable all the time....

I think it's safe to say that the mood inside our homes is probably the most important part of their ambiance. We can have it decorated beautifully and immaculately clean, but as the saying goes, "If Mama ain't happy, ain't nobody happy!" 📖

16. Is there an area of your home that's strictly your husband's to control? If not, where might you make room to allow him this space?

17. Does the physical and emotional ambiance in your home reflect the mood you want to create for yourself and others? If not, what might need to be changed for your home to feel more like a safe haven for your family?

🌿 GROWING TOGETHER
(Sharing the Truth in Small-Group Discussion)

📖 Our marriage was suffering because Greg was feeling the pressure to suppress his true self while I was trying to mold him into my image. I couldn't understand why he couldn't be more like me (outgoing and talkative), and I would drag him to parties and places where he could "practice" being more sociable. He would return home drained, not understanding why I thought it was necessary to try to change his more introverted personality. The problem, of course, wasn't *his*, but mine. 📖

18. Has your marriage suffered because you've tried to mold your husband into the image of who you want him to be? If so, how? If not, how have you safeguarded your relationship from this destructive dynamic?

19. What are the specific things you've tried to change about your husband in the past? In hindsight, were they really worth mentioning? Why or why not?

📖 Women often say they want their husbands to communicate more on an emotional level, but for most men to feel comfortable doing that, they must know we honor their feelings, whether we agree with their assessments or not. If your husband shares his feelings, try not to get angry with him for having them. Again, applaud his courage to confront the issue.

Greg and I were out on a date recently and saw a bumper sticker that read, "Men have feelings too! But then, who cares?" I was saddened by the expression, because I think it says what many men feel, not just because of the world we live in, but because of the women they live with....

Validating someone's feelings is simply a matter of somehow communicating, "I'm not sure I would feel the same way in this situation, but you have a valid right to feel the way you do, and I can respect and appreciate that." Validation is our way of saying to our spouses, "I'm in your corner. I've got your back. I won't twist this knife or use this information against you or think any less of you because you feel this way. If anything, I think more highly of you for trusting me with your feelings." 📖

20. When your husband shares feelings with you that you don't necessarily agree with or appreciate hearing, do you get angry? sad? defensive? Or can you demonstrate to him that you care about his feelings?

21. Describe what it means to validate a person's feelings. How would it feel to be validated by someone you love when you are concerned about something? How would it make you feel to see others validated by your response to them?

📖 Creating a safe haven for my family isn't always easy, and I don't succeed at it on a daily basis. But because I love my husband and kids, I always *desire* to succeed at it. It takes time and energy and focus, but it's a ministry that is very worthy of all these things.

It often helps me to remember that the real me isn't the person whom others see teaching from a stage or speaking in front of a camera. That's the public side of me. The *real* me is the *private* side of me, the person with whom my husband and children have to live. If I minister to the world yet neglect my family's needs or harden their hearts toward me because of how busy I am or how difficult I am to live with, what have I gained? 📖

22. Do you ever treat your husband (or children) in ways that you would be ashamed for others to observe? If so, describe one of those times, what you did, and what you *wish* in hindsight you had done.

23. How can we avoid living a double life—acting sweet as pie when people are watching or listening, but sour as a lemon when no one besides our husband or children are around?

∞

*D*ear God, we confess there are times when we are difficult to live with. Marriage often brings out both the best and the worst in us. Help us in tense times or when we have major differences of opinion to always demonstrate proper respect and to fight our battles fairly so as to foster genuine intimacy, unconditional love, and acceptance in our relationships. Show us how we can create safer havens for our families to grow up in so that our husbands, children, and guests see the lavish love of God operating in our lives, and especially within the walls of our homes. For hearing these prayers, Lord, we give You thanks. Amen.

throwing fuel on his flame (part A)

Read chapters 15 and 16 of *Every Woman's Marriage.*

PLANTING GOOD SEEDS
(Personally Seeking God's Truth)

As you seek to be faithful to your husband, plant these good seeds in your heart:

> You have heard that it was said, "Do not commit adultery."
> But I tell you that anyone who looks at a [man] lustfully has
> already committed adultery with [him] in [her] heart. (Matthew 5:27–28, NIV)

> But among you there must not be even a hint of sexual immorality. (Ephesians 5:3, NIV)

> God wants you to be holy, so you should keep clear of all sexual
> sin. Then each of you will control your body and live in holiness
> and honor—not in lustful passion as the pagans do, in their ignorance of God and his ways. (1 Thessalonians 4:3–5)

1. Why does God call us to control our own bodies and live in holiness and honor?

Another good seed to plant in our heart is 2 Corinthians 10:3–5 (NIV):

> For though we live in the world, we do not wage war as the world does. The weapons we fight with are not the weapons of the world.... We take captive every thought to make it obedient to Christ.

2. Explain what taking "captive every thought" and making "it obedient to Christ" means.

3. Why is learning to take thoughts captive important for a married woman? Is this something that comes naturally to you? Why or why not?

⚒ WEEDING OUT DECEPTION
(Recognizing the Truth)

📖 Just as a table has four legs that support it, we have four distinct components that comprise our sexuality: the physical, mental, emotional, and spiritual aspects. These four parts combine to form the unique sexual individual who God designed each of us to be. In other words, our sexuality isn't *what we do.* Our sexuality is *who we are,* and we were made with a body, mind, heart, and spirit, not just a body. If one of these legs is neglected, the table gets out of balance and quickly becomes a slide instead. And where might that slide lead? The pit of marital discontent, or even sexual compromise, as we may feel tempted to get one of these four needs met outside of our marriage relationship....

Genuine sexual and emotional fulfillment can only be discovered within a marriage relationship, not through an extramarital fling, solitary masturbation, lustful fantasies of other people, and so on. God designed the perfect plan of one man and one woman coming together in one unshakable union called marriage, where they can be naked and unashamed, just as Adam and Eve were before sin entered the picture and caused them to hide in shame (see Genesis 2:25 and 3:7). 📖

4. Have you ever felt that your husband wasn't meeting one of your basic needs, whether that need was physical, mental, emotional, or spiritual? If so, were you tempted to feel justified in looking outside your marriage to have that need met? Why or why not?

5. How can you safeguard yourself from giving in to this temptation in the future?

📖 Many women think that our emotional desires are by far superior to our husbands' sexual desires. We view our needs for emotional connection as legitimate and good. After all, God is exceedingly loving and wants relational intimacy with us. But we may have a hard time imagining that a man's need for sexual connection is just as legitimate and good. And that's where our theology goes awry.

Your husband, and all men, are made in the image of God, and God declared His creation "very good." Did God know Adam and all his male descendants would be visually stimulated and crave physical touch? would so deeply desire frequent and passionate sexual encounters? Yes. God designed men to be this way, and we cannot call unholy that which God has created and called good.

I can't explain this mystery, but I believe that when we get to heaven we'll say "Aha!" when we are able to understand the connection between male sexuality and God's spirituality. In the meantime, we must believe that the wife's role as the sole source of her husband's sexual satisfaction is a high and holy calling. 📖

6. Do you see your role in fulfilling your husband's sexual desires as a "high and holy calling"? Why or why not?

7. Have you ever felt as if your emotional needs were superior to your husband's physical needs? If so, how did it affect your relationship?

📖 When Greg gave me such a sweet compliment about how I light his fire by letting him look at me so often, I responded, "I'll bet you'll love looking at me a lot more when I lose these extra ten pounds!" He looked at my body and said, "Shannon, I can't imagine that you could ever look more beautiful to me than you do right now."

There's a powerful, liberating message in Greg's words, girlfriends. We can't let a few extra vanity pounds cause such inhibition that we rob our husbands of one of the things he craves most—visual stimulation. Your husband is not as concerned with your dress size as he is with your willingness to let him look at you in (and out of) that dress. Most husbands will tell you that they don't need or even want their wives to look like anorexic celebrities. They want to gaze upon their wives' curves, regardless of their size. Your husband wants you to feel good enough about yourself that you are willing without hesitation to let him drink you in through his eyes any time he wants. 📖

8. Does the phrase "naked and unashamed" describe how you feel about yourself in your bedroom? Does it bother you that your husband longs to gaze upon your nude body? Why or why not?

9. What things can you do to foster a more uninhibited atmosphere in your bedroom? How do you think your husband would react to your taking such measures?

10. Do you feel that being less inhibited in private with your husband is contradictory to being a "good Christian girl"? Why or why not?

🐚 HARVESTING JOY AND PASSION
(Applying the Truth)

📖 Many women tell me that they love their husbands and even enjoy an occasional orgasm, but when their husbands try to initiate sex, these wives are often not all that interested. Some have even confessed that they wish sex wasn't a "requirement" in the relationship because they really don't feel much need for it.

If you've had similar thoughts, let me remind you that God created women, as well as men, to be sexual beings. So even if sexual stimulation and satisfaction aren't as strongly felt needs for you as they are for your husband, they *are* needs you have. Perhaps these needs are deeply buried or masked in you, but they're there nonetheless.

There have certainly been times when Greg was interested in having sex, but I wasn't mentally prepared for it. I would entertain the thought in my brain for a second or two, just to see if I could muster up any desire whatsoever. If I felt as if I were hitting a wall and couldn't work up enough energy to get over that wall, my response was usually, "No, not tonight," followed by some lame excuse.

However, I have come to understand that a man can take his wife's sexual rejection very personally. It feels as if she's not just saying no to sex but no to him, and no to his love, his attention, his affection, and his desire for connection with her. I also discovered

that even if I felt no desire whatsoever at the moment Greg initiated, desire would quickly blossom if I engaged in certain sexual
activities out of love for him and out of my desire to receive the
love he wanted to give me. In other words, I can choose to scale
the wall instead of allowing it to keep me from the oneness that
Greg and I can experience.

And what do I usually find on the other side of that wall?
Euphoria. Some of our most intensely pleasurable moments have
been experienced during times when my brain had initially told
me I wasn't interested. 📖

11. Can you identify with women who say that they wish sex wasn't a
requirement in the relationship? Have you buried your sexual desires
somewhere so deep within that you don't know how to find them? If
so, what may have been the cause?

12. What would it take for you to *scale* the wall rather than *hit* the wall the
next time your husband initiates sex? Is it possible that your body could
learn to enjoy that which your mind initially attempts to reject? Why or
why not?

📖 When you are aware of how your lack of interest in sex can
hurt your husband, it can motivate you to be more sensitive about
how you respond during those times when it's really *not* a good

time. So, rather than a cut-and-dried no, consider a more promising reply, such as, "This is not a good time for me right now, but can we carve out some time in the morning or tomorrow night? or this weekend?" Let your husband know that you are interested in connecting passionately with him (ideally within the next day or so), but that you prefer to wait until a more opportune time so that you can be more mentally and emotionally present or physically energized. Then make that time a priority, just as you would want him to make a date night with you a priority. Rather than perceiving this as procrastination or rejection, your husband will feel honored by your conscious effort to seize a more opportune moment in the near future for a passionate physical connection with him. Then he will melt when you make yourself ready and *you're* the one doing the initiating. 📖

13. When it's not a good time for you to engage in sexual relations, does your husband generally get a "no" response from you or a "yes, but not right now" response? How do you think your typical response makes him feel?

14. Do you believe that your husband's sexual needs are just as legitimate to him and his sense of well-being as your emotional needs are to you? Why or why not?

15. Do you appreciate that your husband finds you sexually attractive? How can you show him that you value his sexual interest in you? Think of at least three tangible ways to express your sentiments, and circle one that you intend to do within the next week.

❧ Growing Together
(Sharing the Truth in Small-Group Discussion)

📖 [Men] want to feel special and welcomed when making love. They want their wives to sexually desire them.

When a wife loses interest, her husband feels shortchanged. It's really no different than how a woman can feel shortchanged by her husband when he seems disinterested in meeting her emotional needs. Meeting each other's needs, both sexual and emotional, is definitely a two-way street. Our husbands want us to be as excited and passionate about fulfilling their sexual needs as we want them to be about fulfilling our emotional needs.

As I've sought to become a more eager sexual partner for Greg, I've had to learn that sexuality comprises four unique components that are intricately intertwined. I've discovered that by pursuing a physical connection with him, I'm opening the door to a more intimate emotional, mental, and spiritual connection with him as well. This revelation has helped me look forward to our lovemaking as much as I look forward to walking, talking, or worshiping with him. I've been delighted to find that my eagerness to connect with Greg physically has inspired him to connect with me on the other levels as well. 📖

16. Do you look forward to making love with your husband as much as you look forward to walking, talking, dining, or worshiping with him? Why or why not?

17. Would your husband describe you as an eager sex partner? Why or why not?

    📖 It's been said that for a woman, sexual pleasure and orgasm are 95 percent mental and 5 percent physical, emphasizing the key role that mental preparation plays in women's lovemaking. While no one can assign an exact percentage to the importance that each component plays in creating a pleasurable sexual response, I believe it's true that preparing yourself mentally can result in more frequent and incredibly satisfying sexual encounters. 📖

18. What thoughts might a woman entertain to better prepare herself to fulfill her husband's sexual needs? (For example, what might she wear to bed, what kind of music might she play at bedtime, what could she offer to do to help him relax?)

19. What thoughts might she want to avoid as she anticipates moments alone with her husband? (For example, worrying about the cleanliness of the house or what she faces at work the next day, rehearsing how she wants to confront him about certain issues once they are alone.)

📖 Now consider two types of sexual connection in marriage— *light-bulb sex* versus *laser-beam sex*. We engage in light-bulb sex when we spread our mental and physical energies in many different directions (such as toward the kid who needs to be disciplined, the laundry that needs to be washed, the friend we need to call, how much we wish we could get "this" over with, and so on) rather than focusing on our husbands. Such a connection may satisfy the immediate physical urge for sexual release, but its power to bond a couple together mentally, emotionally, and spiritually is greatly limited.

With laser-beam sex, however, both spouses concentrate their mental and physical energies on each other.... They strive to meet each other's unique needs for physical and emotional intimacy. They make time for sexual intimacy a priority, even scheduling time alone together especially for this purpose, if necessary. They are physically and mentally present with each other, fully experiencing the intoxicating moments of pleasure and comfort with their mate.

Doesn't laser-beam sex sound much more appealing and ultimately satisfying to you than light-bulb sex? Sure. And which do you think would ignite more joy and passion in your husband? No doubt, he'd love to have you mentally, as well as physically, present during lovemaking. There's nothing more satisfying than knowing that you are the center of attention in your mate's mind, especially during sexual moments together. 📖

20. What distracting thoughts fill your mind when you are trying to focus on being intimate with your mate? What could you do to settle those issues so that they don't become distractions during times of intimacy with your mate?

21. Have you and your husband ever scheduled time alone, strictly for the purpose of making love? Does this sound like something you'd enjoy doing? Why or why not?

22. Think of at least five (ten if you are feeling inspired!) adjectives that would describe how your husband would feel if you initiated sex more often or demonstrated that you are eager to be sexually intimate with him.

23. Now think of at least five or more adjectives that would describe how it would make *you* feel to know that you've caused your husband to feel the things you've described. Would experiencing these emotions ignite the joy and passion you both desire?

∞

*H*eavenly Father, it's hard for us to understand the complexity of female sexuality, not to mention the complexity of male sexuality. But we know that Your perfect plan of one man and one woman being committed to each other for life enhances our abilities to be naked and unashamed with each other. Help us aspire to being the sexually eager wives that our husbands long for. Give us wisdom and discernment for how to effectively communicate our needs without ignoring or patronizing our husbands' needs. Unite us together as husbands and wives, not only as one flesh, but also one heart, one mind, and one spirit. In Jesus's name, amen.

throwing fuel on his flame (part B)

Read chapters 17, 18, and 19 of *Every Woman's Marriage*.

🪣 PLANTING GOOD SEEDS
(Personally Seeking God's Truth)

As you seek to establish a deeper level of spiritual and emotional intimacy with your husband, plant this seed in your heart:

> But what happens when we live God's way? He brings gifts into our lives, much the same way that fruit appears in an orchard— things like affection for others, exuberance about life, serenity. We develop a willingness to stick with things, a sense of compassion in the heart, and a conviction that a basic holiness permeates things and people. We find ourselves involved in loyal commitments, not needing to force our way in life, able to marshal and direct our energies wisely. (Galatians 5:22–23, MSG)

Read back through this passage on the fruits of the spirit, underlining those qualities you believe you possess in abundance, and circling those which you'd like to ask the Lord's help in developing more fully.

As you seek to lighten your husband's load by relying more on God, plant these good seeds in your heart:

> I am your shield,
> your very great reward. (Genesis 15:1, NIV)

> Your love, O LORD, reaches to the heavens,
> your faithfulness to the skies.
> Your righteousness is like the mighty mountains,
> your justice like the great deep....
> How priceless is your unfailing love!
> Both high and low...
> find refuge in the shadow of your wings.
> They feast on the abundance of your house;
> you give them drink from your river of delights.
> (Psalm 36:5–8, NIV)

1. While a husband should meet many of his wife's emotional needs, why are wives sometimes tempted to place *all* the responsibility on their husbands' shoulders rather than looking to God for the love and attention they crave? Is this sometimes a temptation for you? Why or why not?

⚒ WEEDING OUT DECEPTION
(Recognizing the Truth)

> 📖 Greg and I had been married less than five years when I volunteered to be a summer camp counselor. I went to the camp expect-

ing to get swept up in serving the needs of the teenagers. However, I got swept up in an inappropriate emotional fling with Scott, a single male counselor.

I am sure you are wondering how I could have let that happen. In my midtwenties and incredibly naive about the dynamics of emotional affairs, I honestly thought that my actions were completely pure because Scott and I were not doing anything "sexual." We worshiped together during the evening services. We led Bible studies together with our coed small groups. We talked intimately about spiritual issues, sharing our favorite encouraging scriptures. We prayed together, holding hands only because we thought that's what people should do when they pray. As the week went on, the battle in my mind began to rage. Scott felt far more like a new boyfriend than a brother in Christ. Going home to Greg felt like a letdown.

A few days later, Scott began showing up at my house to spend his afternoons off with me while Greg was at work. It wasn't until Scott and I wound up in each other's arms that it dawned on us both that our feelings for one another had crossed the line, that confessions had to be made to my husband, and that new boundary lines had to be drawn in the relationship to avoid further inappropriate involvement. That's when I realized that there is a powerful connection between spirituality and sexuality. 📖

2. Have you shared (or do you currently share) a spiritual bond with another male that could pose a threat to your sexual integrity? If so, how does reading this passage from *Every Woman's Marriage* make you feel about the situation?

3. What types of spiritual activities do you think married women should avoid engaging in with men other than their husbands? Why?

    📖 Don't let past sin intimidate you into a life of shame and sexual disconnection. We all have our own unique struggles (whether they are spiritual, mental, emotional, or physical). Husbands and wives have to learn how to fight battles *together* rather than allowing them to create turmoil in the relationship. The key to fighting together instead of fighting each other is being honest with yourself and with each other, freely forgiving each other, covering each other's back, and spurring each other on toward victory. When you experience overwhelming temptations that pose threats to your marital oneness, who better to ask accountability from than the person who has a vested interest in your ability to overcome that issue?

    Yes, in taking off your mask, you run the risk of losing your husband's respect if he fails to understand your struggle or if he takes it too personally. But you also stand to gain his respect and deeper levels of spiritual connection and sexual intimacy when you no longer have to pretend to be someone you are not. Knowing that Greg is aware of all the ugly stuff in my past yet is still by my side in the present and looking forward to a continued future together gives me a great sense of safety and security. It also makes me want to give him the gift of my body as an expression of my love for him. 📖

4. Make a list of at least three pros and cons to living a completely open-book life with your spouse, involving him in even your deepest, darkest struggles.

Pros   Cons

5. Now take a step back and look at the big picture. Do you have more to gain or more to lose by being real in your marriage relationship? Do you believe genuine intimacy is worth the risk? Why or why not?

📖 As we've seen, sex can be a powerful tool, and while some husbands may enjoy being bribed in such a way, using sex to manipulate someone was never God's intention. To have a healthy relationship, a wife needs to offer sex with no strings attached, out of love and commitment rather than as a bargaining tool.

One possible reason for this dynamic is that when a woman is single and dating, she has a certain power over a man. She knows, *I've got something you want, and I'll decide when you can have it.* In withholding sex until the honeymoon, she uses her sexual power in a beneficial and godly way. However, after the vows are exchanged, this mentality needs to change. She needs to embrace the idea that *I've got something you want, and because I love you and I've committed to being your wife and your sole source of sexual satisfaction, you can have it whenever you'd like.* Of course, I'm not talking about being a sexual doormat to be walked all over without any concern for her needs or personal boundaries. I'm simply saying that sex is to be offered freely in a marriage relationship, not used as bribery. 📖

6. Have there been times when you offered your husband sex with strings attached, hoping to bribe him into giving you something you want? If so, how does that make you feel in hindsight?

7. If your husband spent quality time with you to bribe you into being willing to do something he wanted you to do, how might you respond? Might a husband have the right to feel the same way if his wife uses sex as a means of manipulating him into satisfying her own agenda? Why or why not?

🐚 HARVESTING JOY AND PASSION
(Applying the Truth)

📖 Of course, Greg wasn't always up to talking and praying at great length every time he desired sex. Maybe your husband has expressed a similar preference—that he doesn't want to *talk*, but rather *touch*. Perhaps he doesn't want to *pray*, he just wants to *play*. In those times, I've found that it helps to combine the two activities—playing and praying.

For example, as you and your husband come together, you can silently pray, *Lord, I may not feel like doing this right now, but I offer sex with my husband as an act of worship before You.* As you begin to rub his chest, visualize what's behind that rugged exterior and pray (sometimes aloud, sometimes silently), *Lord, thank You for my husband's heart. Thank You that he loves me so much, that he finds me attractive, and that he desires to be sexual with me.* As you become one in the flesh, silently pray, *Lord, thank You that You have knit us together as husband and wife. Help us remain true to our commitments to You and to each other. Strengthen us as a couple and help us to be in one accord.*

You get the idea. If the spiritual and emotional connection is what you are craving and the physical connection is what he is craving, swirl the two together and both of you can go to sleep satisfied. 📖

8. Based on what you have read in *Every Woman's Marriage,* is there a big distinction between sexual and spiritual intimacy in marriage? Is one more holy than the other? Should a wife feel offended when her husband would rather play than pray? Why or why not?

9. Do you find the idea of combining *playing* and *praying* foreign or familiar? How might this combination be beneficial in a marriage?

📖 Several husbands said that their wives seemed to pick and choose which scriptures they obeyed. These wives are into the verses "love your neighbor" and "husbands, love your wives as Christ loved the church," but they often ignore the second half of the verse: "The husband should not deprive his wife of sexual intimacy, which is her right as a married woman, nor should the wife deprive her husband" (1 Corinthians 7:3) and "The wife gives authority over her body to her husband" (verse 4). These husbands expressed frustration—and understandably so. After all, sexual intimacy is God's idea. It is not dirty or worldly. Sexual intimacy, according to God's design, is the most powerful way that two humans can connect with each other. When a husband and wife come together and become one through sexual intimacy in the presence of God, they are reflecting the nature of the Trinity. When couples view sex as sacred, it can become a wonderful act of worship. 📖

10. Explain how sexual intimacy within marriage can be an act of worship to God.

11. Do you agree with the scriptural mandate for husbands and wives not to withhold sexual pleasure from one another? Why or why not?

📖 It's admirable for a woman to be actively involved in her local church. It's good for her to be hands-on in her children's lives, to fulfill various social roles and responsibilities, and to have a career if she so chooses. However, if the combination of all those things causes you to have no energy left over for sexual intimacy with your husband, then you're too busy. Consider scaling back your

office hours or dropping out of a church committee or two so that
you can make more time and have more energy to minister to your
husband's sexual needs. Sex isn't a secular act that we squeeze in
between our spiritual activities. It's one of the most important spiritual activities in existence—and you alone can rightfully fill that
role. A wife is the only human on the planet whom God has
ordained to satisfy her husband's sexual needs. What a unique
opportunity we have been given to minister to our husbands in
such a powerful way! 📖

12. Do you consider your husband's sexual needs a ministry worthy of your
time and attention? Why or why not?

13. What optional things in your life drain you of time and energy that you
could be pouring into your sexual relationship with your husband? Are
you willing to reevaluate your priorities and let some things go for the
sake of your marriage? Why or why not?

📖 Remember the big blowout I wrote about in the opening of
this book? I was contemplating leaving Greg and our two young
children in search of the love I felt entitled to when I tearfully
exclaimed, "You just don't meet my emotional needs!" But Greg
saw past my weaknesses to my genuine needs and sincerely replied,
"Shannon, you have a Grand Canyon of emotional needs, and
even if every man in Dallas lined up outside your doorstep to

spend time with you, it wouldn't be enough! *Until you look to God to satisfy your emotional needs,* there's nothing that I, or any other man on the planet, can do to satisfy you!"

While some women may have taken this as a major insult and walked out the door, I recognized the truth in his statement. In all honesty, it was actually a relief to hear. I had given lots of men opportunities to meet my emotional needs, and the idea that God could meet them gave me a glimmer of hope. 📖

14. Does the phrase "Grand Canyon of emotional needs" strike a chord in you? Do you have emotional needs that don't ever seem to be fulfilled? Why or why not?

15. Do you agree that God is the only One who can meet *all* of your emotional needs? Why or why not? If so, write about a specific need you asked Him to meet and how He met that need in your life.

16. What effect would it have on your husband to know that you are lightening his load and looking to God to meet your emotional needs instead of demanding that your husband meet all of them? How can you give your husband this kind of gift?

❧ GROWING TOGETHER
(Sharing the Truth in Small-Group Discussion)

> 📖 In the earlier years of our marriage, neither Greg nor I under-
> stood the importance of making a spiritual and emotional connec-
> tion rather than just a physical one. There were many times that I
> thought I had married a sex addict, and Greg probably thought he
> had married a frigid prude.
>
> How did we formulate these opinions? Because by the time I
> got my clothes and makeup off, brushed my teeth, and climbed
> under the covers, Greg's motor was already running. He'd look at
> me with a hopeful grin and say, "You want to have sex?" For him,
> the desire to have sex seemed to come out of nowhere, whereas the
> thought wouldn't have even crossed my mind. Without the oppor-
> tunity to warm up to the idea, I responded coldly to the invitation.
> I would usually reply, "No, just hold me and let's talk." Most of
> those times when he tried to initiate again before going to sleep,
> I felt irritated or hurt that he didn't respect my earlier no. 📖

17. Do you think it is reasonable for a wife to expect that her husband
    should be able to "just cuddle" frequently without any hope or expec-
    tation of a sexual connection? Why or why not?

18. Should a woman be offended or flattered when her husband finds her
    sexually inviting? Why do you feel the way you do?

📖 While it's important to enjoy sex only according to God's plan and to avoid the scripturally forbidden acts mentioned earlier in the chapter, couples don't need to be legalistic about what's proper in the bedroom between husband and wife. While some Christians jokingly say that the only appropriate way for a couple to have intercourse is with the lights off and in the missionary position, they have no biblical basis for this position. (Pun intended!) Some Christians also believe that oral sex is an unholy act, but this opinion has no scriptural basis. In fact, the Song of Solomon has numerous references to oral pleasures and in no way condemns the act.

As long as a sexual position or technique is not offensive to either partner and is found to be pleasurable, then it's okay as long as it sifts successfully through the six-question grid—Is it prohibited in Scripture? beneficial to the relationship? limited to the married partners? Is it known, and approved of, by your spouse? Does it involve your spouse and bring the two of you together rather than separate you? Any sexual expression is acceptable as long as it successfully meets these criteria. 📖

19. Do you agree with the logic of the six-question grid discussed on pages 173–174 in chapter 18 of *Every Woman's Marriage*? Why or why not?

20. Why do you think that Christians have considered so many sexual activities taboo, even within marriage?

📖 There's much more to sexual intimacy than intercourse. Physical pleasure should be the dessert enjoyed after the appetizer of appreciation, the entrée of encouragement and unconditional love, and the side dish of respect. Any man who is starved of those things and only given dessert will eventually become an undernourished husband. 📖

21. Do you agree that even if a man has all the sex he wants, he'll be undernourished if he feels unappreciated, discouraged, or disrespected? Why or why not?

22. On a scale of 1 to 10 (1 being undernourished and 10 being incredibly healthy), how do you think your husband would rate the appreciation, encouragement, unconditional love, respect, and sexual pleasure he receives from you? Why?

23. What would it take on your part for your husband to increase his rating for you by at least one notch? two notches? Are you willing to try to move his rating in that direction?

📖 If we can learn to ignite the joy and passion that both husbands and wives desire in marriage, imagine the effect that this will have not just in our own families, but on society as a whole. There would be less stress and a much greater sense of peace in our homes. Divorce rates could decline drastically. Children would grow up in two-parent homes with the security of knowing that Mom and Dad really love each other. As a result, they would not be as tempted to turn to gangs, drugs, alcohol, cutting, or other pain-numbing activities. Young people would see that sex is worth waiting for until marriage because adults would be modeling healthy, happy, passion-filled relationships. As a result, premarital pregnancy and abortion rates would be reduced and sexually transmitted diseases could be far less of a social and economic concern.

These principles are the best way to affair-proof and divorce-proof marriages, the best way for families to live in harmony with one another, and the best way for children to grow up in homes where they learn to respect, love, and cherish others, including, some day, their own spouses.

If we can embrace and strive to apply these principles, passing these values down to future generations, we could inspire a whole new, more wonderful world in which to live—a world where marriage is once again a sacred, celebrated institution, where children can feel safe and secure, and where the lavish love of Christ is evident in our hearts and in our homes. 📖

24. Have you ever felt that you can't change society or that there isn't much that you alone can do to help our world become a better place? Why have you felt the way you have?

25. Does the previous excerpt give you hope that you can have a positive influence on society simply by making your own marriage stronger? Why or why not?

26. What strategies for igniting joy and passion in your marriage inspired you the most as you read *Every Woman's Marriage*? If you implemented them, what effect could it have on your life? your husband's life? your kids' lives? society as a whole?

∞

Dear Lord, You've given us far more power than we've ever realized. Not only do You allow us to control our own destinies, but You allow us to impact the destinies of many other lives as well, simply by the choices we make. If we focus on our marriage relationships as one of our top priorities, many people stand to benefit from the positive ripple effects. On the other hand, many people stand to suffer from the negative ripple effects of divorce. Strengthen us, Lord, to be the wives You desire us to be. Grant us wisdom and discernment in creating marriage relationships that truly bring You glory. For it is not only our personal joy that we seek, nor that of our husbands, but we also seek Your joy as we know You take pleasure in watching us strive to become more and more like You. In Jesus's most holy and precious name we pray, amen.

don't keep it to yourself

Congratulations on finishing this workbook! I pray that in addition to learning how to avoid extinguishing your husband's flame for you, you've also gleaned many ideas on how you can rekindle and even throw fuel on the flame of joy and passion that he carries for you.

If you've benefited from completing this workbook, consider inviting a group of women together and leading them toward discovering how to ignite joy and passion in their marriage relationships as well. This can be a source of encouragement to you, but it will also enable you to encourage and help other women who may be struggling with a lack of contentment in their marriages. When we encourage one another to open up about our struggles and their effects on our marriages, we'll be able to give and receive the support we need to remain wholeheartedly committed to our husbands.

You'll find more information about starting such a group on pages 2–3 in the section "Questions You May Have About This Workbook."

every man resources to help you pursue the marriage of your dreams

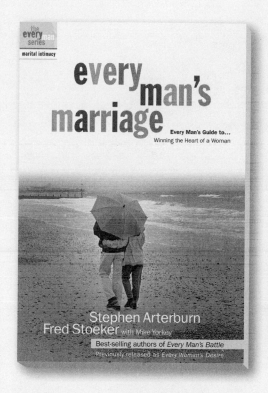
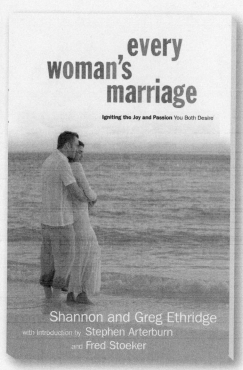
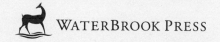

Helping women win the **battle** by **building** a strong **foundation** of **integrity**

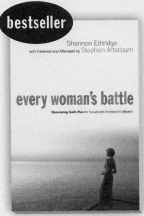

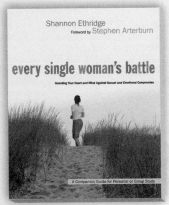

NOW AVAILABLE FROM SHANNON ETHRIDGE MINISTRIES

Does your thirst for love and intimacy seem insatiable? Are you choking on the bitter taste of broken relationships or sexual struggles? Are you ready to taste the Living Water that Jesus offered the Woman at the Well so that she would "never thirst again?"

Experiencing the lavish love of God for yourself is the only way to quench your deep thirst for love and intimacy. *Words of Wisdom for Women at the Well* can help you: recognize the "neon sign" that draws unhealthy men your direction, identify the core issues that pull you into dysfunctional relationships, surrender guilt and shame that lead you to medicate your pain with men, discover the "heavenly affair" that the Lord passionately draws us into, and prepare for stronger, healthier relationships in the future.

౼

Once you've tasted the Living Water that Jesus offers, you'll no longer be a *Woman at the Well*, but a *Well Woman*!

And more than likely, you'll want to do just as the original Woman at the Well did in Samaria after her intimate encounter with Jesus—invite others to taste the life-changing love of Christ!

Through these forty devotions of preparation, *Words of Wisdom for Well Women* will help you: remain faithful in nurturing your own intimate relationship with Christ, plan and conduct powerful *Women at the Well* growth group meetings, empower others to live sexually pure and emotionally fulfilling lives, and begin a new kind of sexual revolution in your corner of the world!